CHRISTIAN
HIGH SCHOOL
RELIGION SERIES

Fitting In

Relationships with God and Others

Student Book

Prepared by: Robert Dosien

CONCORDIA PUBLISHING HOUSE · SAINT LOUIS

Write to Library for the Blind, 1333 S. Kirkwood Road, St. Louis, MO 63122-7295 to obtain *Fitting In* (Student Book) in Braille or sightsaving print for the visually impaired.

3558 S. Jefferson Avenue, St. Louis, MO 63118-3968
Manufactured in the United States of America

9 10 11 12 13 14 15 16 09 08 07

Contents

To the Student

"Mom! Mom! I can't wear these pants! They look like 'high-water pants' on me! And my shirt . . . Oh, Mom! The cuffs come halfway to my elbows!"

Have you ever felt like you've grown out of all your clothes? You just don't seem to fit into *anything* anymore?

You might feel the same way about your whole life. You might feel like you don't "fit in" with your same old friends. Maybe you feel "out of it" at church and youth Bible class lately. You're not quite sure where you stand with God. Perhaps you really feel like a misfit in your high school classes. And when you think about your life at home, maybe those puzzle pieces don't fit together quite right either.

Fitting in—that's what this course is all about. How does it feel to "fit in" with God, with others, and with yourself? Through the sessions in this course, you'll discover more about God's love for you, how He helps you develop positive relationships with Him and with others, and how you can trust Him daily to guide you in all your "fitting in."

The Editors

Unit 1

My Relationship with God

Picture an old, ragged patchwork quilt. The sun has faded some of the once-colorful squares. Lots of use and many washings have worn and torn some of the patches. But the handmade quilt, though mended and repatched, still does the job it was made to do. It still keeps someone warm.

In many ways, we are each like a patchwork quilt. God made us each unique. He blessed us each with different gifts—like the variety of colors and patterns in a quilt. And He made us each for a purpose—to serve Him in our own unique ways.

But in one way, we AREN'T like a patchwork quilt. Because Jesus died for us, and because our sins died with Jesus, God makes us "new creatures." He didn't just "patch us" with new patches. He didn't just cover up our sins and hide them! God says, **"Therefore, if anyone is in Christ, he is a new creation; the old has gone, the new has come" (2 Corinthians 5:17).** God loved each of us THAT MUCH! He holds each of us in this grand love. And God wants us each to know His love, trust Him to love, and share His love with everyone around us. Each of us is a "sinner-saint." And God has a special purpose for each of us. By developing a positive self-concept and by enjoying a happy, healthy relationship with God, we can each grow to know and understand His role in—and His purpose for—our lives.

Session 1

Who Am I?

Read the following poem:

ABOUT SCHOOL

(This poem was handed to a grade 12 English teacher in Regina, Saskatchewan. Although it is not known if the student wrote it himself, it is known that he committed suicide two weeks later.)

He always wanted to say things, But no one understood.
He always wanted to explain things. But no one cared.
So he drew.
Sometimes he would just draw and it wasn't anything. He wanted to carve it in stone or write it in the sky.
He would lie out on the grass and look up in the sky and it would be only him and the sky and the things inside that needed saying.
And it was after that, that he drew the picture. It was a beautiful picture. He kept it under the pillow and would let no one see it.
And he would look at it every night and think about it. And when it was dark, and his eyes were closed, he could still see it.
And it was all of him. And he loved it.
When he started school he brought it with him. Not to show anyone, but just to have it with him like a friend.
It was funny about school.
He sat in a square, brown desk like all the other square, brown desks and he thought it should be red.
And his room was a square, brown room. Like all the other rooms. And it was tight and close. And stiff.
He hated to hold the pencil and the chalk, with his arm stiff and his feet flat on the floor, stiff, with the teacher watching and watching.
And then he had to write numbers. And they weren't anything. They were worse than the letters that could be something if you put them together.
And the numbers were tight and square and he hated the whole thing.
The teacher came and spoke to him. She told him to wear a tie like all the other boys. And he didn't like them and she said it didn't matter.
After that they drew. And he drew all yellow and it was the way he felt about morning. And it was beautiful.
The teacher came and smiled at him. "What's this?" she said. "Why don't you draw something like Ken's drawing?
Isn't that beautiful?"
It was all questions.
After that his mother bought him a tie and he always drew airplanes and rocket ships like everyone else.
And he threw the old picture away.
And when he lay out alone looking at the sky, it was big and blue and all of everything, but he wasn't anymore.
He was square inside and brown, and his hands were stiff, and he was like anyone else. And the thing inside him that needed saying didn't need saying anymore.
It had stopped pushing. It was crushed. Stiff.
Like everything else.

HOW DO I FEEL?

1. What pressures do you find in the poem that take away this person's uniqueness? ______________

____

2. What else did you hear as you read the poem?

____

3. Can you identify with any of the feelings the poem's author had? Which ones?______________

____

4. Do you ever feel boxed in, overlooked, stifled, or crushed? When, and how? ______________

____

5. Who are some people in Scripture who felt boxed in, overlooked, cloned, or pressured to conform?

____

____

WHO AM I?

Write the special words from these Scripture verses that tell what God did for you and help you know more clearly who you are:

Jeremiah 1:5 ______________________________

____

Isaiah 44:2 ______________________________

____

Ephesians 1:4 ______________________________

____

GOD DELIGHTS IN ME

1. Read **Psalm 16:3, John 15:9,** and **Romans 8:31-32.**

According to these verses, how does God feel about you?

____

____

2. How do you feel, knowing God feels so positively about you?

____

GOD MADE ME HIS CHILD

Billions of snowflakes may fall during a snowstorm, but no two are exactly alike. Nor has God ever created another person just like you! No one looks like you look, feels like you feel, or sees things the way you see them. You are one-of-a-kind. You're a precious original—not a copy of someone else. God loves you because He made you. You're one of His "works." He loves you because you're YOU. You're special in His sight. **Psalm 139:14** expresses David's thankful, happy response to God, and we can tell Him the same:

I will praise You because I am fearfully and wonderfully made; Your works are wonderful, I know that full well.

Do you know what a full-of-wonder creation you are? Isn't it neat to know that God is happy that you are you!

Write a short paragraph. Tell how you feel about yourself and your relationship with God.

____

____

____

____

____

A prayer to pray today: *Dear God, You gave me my heart and You gave me my mind. You gave me my smile and You gave me my feelings. You made me in a wonderful way. I thank You, Father, for making me ME! Amen.*

I will praise You because I am fearfully and wonderfully made; Your works are wonderful, I know that full well.

Psalm 139:14

Session 2

God Loves ME??

Shout for joy to the Lord, all the earth. Serve the Lord with gladness; come before Him with joyful songs. Know that the Lord is God. It is He who made us, and we are His; we are His people, the sheep of His pasture. . . . Give thanks to Him and praise His name. For the Lord is good and His love endures forever; His faithfulness continues through all generations.

Psalm 100:1-5

How do you feel when you read **Psalm 100?** Do you feel that God loves you? What does the psalmist say that God has done and will do for you?

____

____

HOW DO I SEE MYSELF?

1. Draw a circle around each sentence that describes how you feel about yourself *most* of the time.

I'm happy.
School bores me.
My parents love me.
I'm a loner.
I am shy and avoid people.
I look forward to going to church and Sunday school on Sunday.
I like to take tests and exams.
I am rather good-looking.
Most people detest me.
I like to learn new things and explore new ideas.
I am a klutz.
I'm a pretty smooth operator.
I feel that I am on the road to success.
I'd rather not go to church anymore, but my parents make me go.
I like to chew gum.
My parents hate me.
I enjoy sports.
I detest television.
My good looks will get me through life.
I enjoy eating ice cream.
I think about the opposite sex a lot.
I consider myself an average, normal teenager.
I'm not sure how my parents feel about me.
I like to meet new people.
I'm often sad.
Going to church is dull, but I go anyway.
I can't stand eating oysters.
Most people like me.
I tend to be a quitter.
A few people think I'm "ugly."
I spend too much time in front of the mirror.
I work hard at developing a good personality.
I daydream a lot.
I dislike sports.
I love Jesus, but I still sin.

2. You've applied for a job. Your potential employer asks you to write a paragraph describing yourself. Write a short paragraph telling about yourself. (Remember, you really want the job!)

____

____

____

____

____

____

____

____

____

HOW DO OTHER PEOPLE SEE ME?

1. Write at least three ways other people might describe you.

____

____

____

2. Ask your parent(s) or adults with whom you live how they see you. Write their answers here.

____

____

____

3. Have a class sharing time. Then write how a classmate described you.

____

____

HOW DOES GOD SEE ME?

1. Now imagine that you're God. (He knows you better than anyone else knows you!) Respond to the descriptions you've given about yourself in the first two parts of this session. How do you think God sees you as He continues to love and care for you? Start your response like this:

Dear ________________(write in your name),

I am aware of the sentences you've circled describing your feelings. I have read your self-description for the job application.

I want to tell you that I ____________________

____

____

____

____

____

____

Love,
God

2. Tell how God sees you according to these passages:

2 Corinthians 5:17 ____________________

John 13:33 __________________________

Galatians 5:13 _______________________

Galatians 3:26 _______________________

Galatians 3:29 _______________________

1 Peter 4:10 _________________________

Ephesians 2:4-6 ______________________

Ephesians 2:10 _______________________

Look at how many wonderful ways God sees you! He loves you exactly the way you are. He loves and forgives you, even when you feel unlovable! You never have to worry that God doesn't love you!

YES, GOD LOVES ME!

By now, you should be able to better understand God's love for you and His acceptance of you as His child, His wonderful creation.

1. How do you know God loves you? Look up these Bible passages and write the ways God shows His love for you.

Matthew 21:22 _______________________

Matthew 28:20 _______________________

Luke 2 ______________________________

John 3:16 ___________________________

John 14:16-17 ________________________

John 14:19 ___________________________

John 14:27 ___________________________

1 Corinthians 10:13 ____________________

Ephesians 1:7 _________________________

2. **Read Romans 5:8.** What *special way* did God demonstrate His love for you?

____

____

Do you remember singing "Jesus loves me, this I know, for the Bible tells me so. . . . " when you were younger? You know from God's Word how much He loves you. He also tells you of His love through all of His creation and through the people—family and friends—He's given to you.

You can add to the song, "Jesus loves me, this I know, we all tell each other so!" Evidence of God's love for you is everywhere!

A prayer to pray today: *Dear God, You show me in so many ways that You love me! I thank and praise you for Your love and care. Help me to remember Your love for me each day, especially when I feel like nobody loves me! I'm glad I can count on You, God!*

Christ Jesus came into the world to save sinners—of whom I am the worst.

1 Timothy 1:15

Session 3

So, God Loves Me—Do I Love Myself?

"I can't get a date! I can't make my parents happy! I can't get good grades! I can't fix my car!" Gregory Glump is gloomy. He hates himself because of all the things he CAN'T do and CAN'T be.

"I can't be a cheerleader! I can't find a job! I can't get into the 'in group' at school! I can't get good grades! I can't be on the track team!" Exhausted Elaine is exasperated. She hates herself because she tries SO HARD to do things like the other kids and be more like them. She just CAN'T keep up with everyone and everything they're doing!

God loves Gregory and Elaine and He accepts them the way they are. Do you think they love themselves? Do they even LIKE themselves?

Did you ever feel like Gregory and Elaine? Do you love yourself? CAN you love yourself? This is a heavy subject! Let's see what it involves.

GOD MADE ME—I'M NOT JUNK!

1. What does **Ephesians 2:10** tell you about what you are? ____________________

____

2. Describe briefly how God sees you **(2 Corinthians 5:17).**

____

____

You have read and learned a lot in the two previous sessions about God's love for you and your relationship with Him. Knowing and accepting His love builds the foundation of your feelings for all parts of your life.

Does knowing that God loves and forgives you make you happy and extra-thankful? Draw your happy face in the margin! Now go on to more heavy stuff.

SOMETIMES I HATE MYSELF—I CAN'T DO ANYTHING RIGHT!

1. Tell some reasons you sometimes hate yourself.

Write short phrases or sentences. Be prepared to talk about these in class.

____

____

____

____

2. Read about some of God's people from Bible times. How did each of these people feel about themselves? How did God feel about each person? How did God show His love to each one?

Adam and Eve **(Genesis 3)**

____

Cain **(Genesis 4:5-16)**

____

Noah **(Genesis 6:8-9; 6:22; 8:15-17; 9:1-17)**

____

Moses **(Exodus 4:10-17)**

____

Hannah **(1 Samuel 1:10-20; 27-28)**

____

Saul **(Acts 8:3; 9:1-22)**

____

3. Finish these thoughts in your own words. Be ready to share more feelings with the class.

I feel like I'm not good enough when

I feel like running away when

I hurt a lot when

I feel different from everyone else when

I feel so lonely when

4. Sometimes people feel so badly about themselves, they forget that God loves them. They forget that God has gifted them with their lives, especially their NEW LIVES through Jesus Christ. They lose their joy in living. They don't know how to love themselves. They think about committing suicide to get rid of all their terrible problems. Is committing suicide really a way out? Does it solve any problems?

Walls, walls, more walls. Walls with doors. Doors without doorknobs. Windows barred. The walls move in on me, inch by inch. Nobody knows I'm here. Nobody cares. I'm trapped. Nobody knows. Nobody cares. I can't take this anymore. Maybe if I kill myself everything will stop closing in on me. Somebody will notice me. I need peace and quiet. Help. Help.

What would you say to a friend who felt so desperate that he or she thought of committing suicide?

What Scripture passages would you use in your own words to help your friend learn to love himself or herself? to remind him or her of God's love?

If Christ is in you, your body is dead because of sin, yet your spirit is alive because of righteousness (Romans 8:10). This passage reminds us that Jesus took all our sins—those we've done and those we will still do—to the cross with Him. He took them away so that we can live anew. Because Christ lives in us, we will want to **LIVE** with Him, in Him, and for Him.

GOD HELPS ME—I CAN LOVE MYSELF!

1. Read **2 Corinthians 3:5.** How does this passage make you feel?

2. Jesus commands us to do something in **John 15:9-17.** Whom are we to love?

Think about God's command. Jesus, your Best Friend, gave His life for you. Because of His loving action, He lives in you, and you live a new life in Christ. Therefore, when you love Jesus, you also love yourself. When you love yourself, you also love Jesus. And—a third dimension—only when you love yourself can you love others around you!

Jesus makes this all possible!

YES—I DO LOVE MYSELF!

1. Write God a love letter on a separate piece of paper. You'll be prayer-writing, communicating your love thoughts to Him.

2. Next, write yourself a love letter. Begin with "Dear (your name)." Tell yourself what assets you have. Don't be stingy! Describe some characteristics you'd like to develop in positive ways.

3. Finally, pretend you're a teen facing a physical or emotional problem. Tell what happens to you and how you succeed in conquering your problem. Be prepared to share your story with the class.

A prayer to pray today: *Dear God, You love me SO MUCH! Sometimes I think only about myself and my own problems. I forget too quickly that You always love me and take care of me. Help me remember Your love and grace so that I can love myself more. Help me remember that because You love me, I am able to love others, too. Amen.*

I pray that you, being rooted and established in love, may have power, together with all the saints, to grasp how wide and long and high and deep is the love of Christ, and to know this love that surpasses knowledge—that you may be filled to the measure of all the fullness of God.

Ephesians 3:17-19

Session 4

God Can Use *Me*?

John and his brother Paul fished from the dock at Lake Thunderbird. Just before dark, as they packed their gear to go back to the lodge, the brothers heard a boat's motor roar and they saw a small fishing boat suddenly overturn in the lake. John and Paul quickly borrowed the marina manager's boat and life jackets. In only a few minutes, they sped to the capsized boat and rescued two elderly fishermen. Later in the lodge, when the gentlemen had dried and explained what had happened, they offered John and Paul money as they repeated their thanks. The boys answered, "We're just glad we saw what happened! God gave us the courage and strength to fish you guys out of the lake!"

Julie had been babysitting for the Durand children for a few months. Joel had just celebrated his fourth birthday, and Katie would soon be three. One evening when Mr. and Mrs. Durand came home, Julie asked, "I'm a Sunday school teacher's helper at my church. Do you take Joel and Katie to Sunday school and church anywhere? If not, I'd like to invite you to visit my church. I'd be glad to take them to the nursery class in Sunday school, too!"

We read in **John 13:1-17** how Jesus served His friends by washing their feet. Jesus wants us to follow His example and serve people around us. Does that mean we have to wash their feet? What do you think it means to serve the Lord? How did God use John and Paul? How did Julie serve the Lord? How can God use YOU? In this session, you'll read and learn about ways God can use you as His servant.

EXCUSES, EXCUSES—WHY ME, LORD?

1. Maybe you're thinking, "But I'm the WORST sinner! Why would God want to use me?" List some of the awful things you've done.

___

___

2. Now confess your sins to God. Use this confession (paraphrased from *Lutheran Worship*) or make up your own.

Most merciful God, I confess that I'm by nature sinful and unclean. I've sinned against You in thought, word, and deed. I haven't loved You with my whole heart. I haven't loved my neighbors as myself. I deserve Your eternal punishment. For Jesus' sake, have mercy on me. Forgive me, renew me, and lead me, so that I might be happy in Your will and walk in Your ways to glorify You. Amen.

Finally, read the pastor's words—the absolution.

Almighty God in His mercy has given His Son to die for you and for His sake forgives you all your sins.

How do these words make you feel?

___

GOD GETS YOU READY

1. Read Paul's testimony in Acts 22:3-16. How did God choose Paul to be His servant?

___

What special command did the Lord give Paul **(verses 15-16)**?

___

2. God gets you ready to serve Him by giving you His love and forgiveness through the means of grace—His Holy Word, Baptism and the Lord's Supper. Tell briefly how you feel as a baptized child of God.

___

If you haven't been baptized, tell why you would like to be.

___

___

Talk to your pastor about becoming baptized. If you don't have a pastor or a home church, ask your teacher to help you.

Why is it important to hear and learn God's Word?

___

___

How do you feel after you have received Christ's body and blood in the Lord's Supper?

___

3. What gifts and blessings does God give you that enable you to serve Him?

Romans 3:22-24 ______________________________

Romans 5:5 ______________________________

2 Corinthians 2:10 ______________________________

Galatians 5:1 ______________________________

Ephesians 2:8 ______________________________

Ephesians 6:10-11 ______________________________

GOD SAYS "GO!"

1. What command does Jesus give us according to **John 13:34?**

____

____

2. Read **Matthew 28:19-20.** Write the key words in Jesus' command.

____

What do you think it means to "make disciples"? And how can you use God's blessings as you "go" for Him?

____

____

3. What promise does Jesus give us **(verse 20)?**

____

____

I'M ON THE "J-TEAM"!

1. God CAN use YOU! You're part of the "J-Team"! The team's action involves getting others to also join "Jesus' team." Where do you start? What's your job? First, ask yourself these questions:

What has Jesus done for me?
How do I really feel about Jesus?
How does Jesus help me each day?
Why do I want to be a part of the "J-Team"?

2. Tell how these Scripture passages teach you to share God's love and message of salvation with others.

Ephesians 4:32; 5:1-2 ______________________________

____

Colossians 3:12-17 ______________________________

____

1 John 1:3-4 ______________________________

____

1 John 5:1-4 ______________________________

____

3. The Holy Spirit works faith in you. You are at your own point in your own Christian growth and maturity. Sometimes you might feel like saying, "Be patient with me—God isn't finished with me yet!"

Read **Romans 15:7.** Describe what you CAN do, no matter how "ready" to serve God you might feel.

____

____

4. Words from a contemporary folksong say, "Pass My love around; pick right up and take My brother's hand, and pass My love around. My Word and Truth to you I leave behind; now be My witness to mankind, now be My witness to mankind."

Now write a short paragraph telling how you think God can use you. You might think back to the student's essay, "ABOUT SCHOOL," in session 1. How can God help you witness and pass His love around?

____

____

____

____

____

____

A prayer to pray today: *Dear Jesus, Please use me in the ways You need me. Make me willing to do Your work. Help me be ready through Your Word and through the power of the Holy Spirit. Always keep me on Your team!*

Be devoted to one another in brotherly love. Honor one another above yourselves. Never be lacking in zeal, but keep your spiritual fervor, serving the Lord.

Romans 12:10-11

Session 5

Concluding Activities for Unit 1

Getting to know yourself—and someone else—can be a real adventure! Try to find out more about yourself and where you stand with God and with others. To do this, you'll need to ask yourself some questions. And it's important to answer the questions honestly.

Answer these questions on your own. Then talk about the questions and your answers with a partner.

1. How would you describe yourself as a child, aged 5-10?

2. Describe something you were proud of when you were a young child.

3. What was your childhood nickname? How did you feel about it?

4. If you don't like your given name, what name would you choose?

Why?

5. What's your favorite possession right now?

6. What's your favorite book, and why?

7. What's the best movie you've ever seen, and why?

8. Who's your favorite person in your whole family, and why?

9. Tell why you like your friend(s).

10. Describe yourself as a friend to others.

11. What's your favorite hobby?

12. Approximately how many times do you pray during one week?

13. What's the MOST important thing in your life right now?

14. What one thing is your biggest concern right now?

15. Do you prefer to be alone, to be with other people a lot, or to enjoy a combination of each?

16. What do you look forward to MOST in your life?

Unit 2

Growing in My Devotional Life with God

Ginny and her family backpacked through the Colorado Rockies, photographed twenty-eight rolls of film in fifteen days, and, when they returned home, documented each developed photo in an elaborate album. This family devoted themselves to remembering and sharing, through photographs, their many fun experiences with relatives and friends!

Can you think of something you have been devoted to, or are devoted to now? What does it mean to be devoted to something? Some people are devoted to their dogs; some are devoted to their jobs. You might have heard people say, "She's a devoted mother," or "He's totally devoted to his girl." To devote yourself to something or someone means that you center your attention on that specific thing or person.

Just like Ginny and her family devoted themselves to taking many pictures of their vacation time spent together, you also devote yourself to certain things in your life. In this unit, you'll be discovering more about yourself and your personal life, especially your devotional life with God.

Session 6

Personal Devotions

How do you feel when you're all alone?

What kinds of things do you do when you're alone?

How often do you take time for your thoughts to center only on God and your relationship to Him?

Why is it important to commit yourself to a time of private devotions—a special time for you to communicate with God?

Why is it important to ask, "How do I start devoting?"

WHY DEVOTE MYSELF TO GOD?

Write the important reasons these passages give for devoting yourself to the Lord.

Ephesians 5:18-20 ______________________________

____

Ephesians 6:18 ______________________________

____

Philippians 1:9 ______________________________

____

Philippians 2:10-11 ______________________________

____

Philippians 4:4-7 ______________________________

____

Colossians 4:2 ______________________________

____

1 Thessalonians 5:16-18 ______________________________

____

MY PERSONAL DEVOTION COMMITMENT

Describe a time period and a location that you could comfortably use for your personal devotions. Are you willing to seriously commit yourself to reading God's Word and talking with Him regularly at some of those times and in some of those places? If so, draw a cross beside those you think are best for you.

____

____

____

____

____

HOW DO I DEVOTE? WHERE DO I START?

You've discovered from the Scripture passages that through personal devotions—your one-to-one communicating with God—God and you can do many things together! You can praise and thank God, ask Him for your needs, ask Him for special requests, confess your sins, and worship Him. God will fill you with the Holy Spirit, give you blessings of the Spirit, and continue to love and care for you and provide you with what you need.

Begin celebrating your life, experiencing joy with your companion and friend, Jesus. Use the following steps as a suggested form for personal devotions.

1. Read a psalm or section of Scripture. You might choose **Psalm 100** or **Psalm 103.**

2. Think about the passage(s) you read. Meditate briefly on what the Scripture means for you.

3. If you chose to read either psalm suggested, then you could, as a personal activity, chart your own life-timeline, either mentally or on paper. Think of joyful times in your life from your birth to the present. When have you been the most joyful? Are you happiest when you are with other people? Joy and gladness—living celebrations—often happen when you're with others. It's a good feeling to know you're not alone. It's also assuring to feel that others consider you unique and special!

4. Read **Luke 15:3-7** (the parable of the lost sheep) and think about the many reasons for joy and celebration in this story Jesus told. Ask yourself, "When does God feel joy? When do I feel joy? What are some ways

I could share my joy and friendship with unhappy people I know?"

5. Sing a favorite song of praise and thanksgiving.

6. Pray from your heart a personal message to God. If you can't think of what to say, make this your personal prayer today: *Dear Jesus, I'm happy and thankful that You died and rose to take my sins away. I can celebrate my life each day because You love me. Help me be a friend to someone who doesn't know You and Your love. Help me share my joy and happiness with others. In Your name I pray. Amen.*

MY DEVOTION PLAN

1. Choose three Scripture passages or chapters to read and meditate for your next three personal devotions.

List the references and tell the theme of each.

2. Recall and write the names of three of your favorite songs that tell you of God's love or in some way help you celebrate joy in Jesus.

3. Create your own personal prayer. You might write a general beginning prayer you could pray each time you devote, allowing you to add special thanks and requests at the end, according to your daily situations and needs. Remember to pray for your own special needs, for your family members and friends, for little things and for big things!

You've now chosen three personal parts for your own private devotions. Will you promise to use them? And will you remain committed to giving the Lord your personal devotion regularly? Remember that wherever you are, in whatever you're doing, you can "think" devotion to God—or read and pray and sing your devotion aloud—or shout out your devotion! Celebrate life through devotion to the Lord!

At the name of Jesus every knee should bow, in heaven and on earth and under the earth, and every tongue confess that Jesus Christ is Lord, to the glory of God the Father.

Philippians 2:10-11

Devote yourselves to prayer, being watchful and thankful.

Colossians 4:2

Be joyful always; pray continually; give thanks in all circumstances, for this is God's will for you in Christ Jesus.

1 Thessalonians 5:16-18

Session 7

Group Devotions

Jesus told His disciples and friends that where two or three gather in His name, He is also there with them. Getting together with others on a regular basis to study and discuss God's Word can deepen your own personal relationship with God as well as help you better understand His Word.

Your worship group might be your family, your teen friends, or a mixed group. You might include in your devotions a Scripture reading, a discussion and insight-sharing time about the Scripture, prayer requests, prayers for each other, and the singing of meaningful, uplifting songs or hymn stanzas.

Who will lead your devotions? Designate someone to be the leader. That same person might be the "whistle-blower" (the one who keeps everyone on the subject and within your set devotion time). Your leader prepares for devotions. He or she reads the Scripture before the group meets, thinks of a few discussion questions about the devotion theme, and chooses related activities, prayers, and songs. A good leader prepares, waits patiently for response to discussion questions, and shows and encourages love and respect for each member of the devotion group.

Encourage each other as members of your devotion "family" to share insights and observations about Scripture readings and what God's Word means to you for your daily living. Encourage each other to share times of joy, sadness, thanksgiving, and hurt. Participate in share-prayers, taking each other's needs to God while meeting as a group and also while you're devoting privately. Support those people who pray spontaneously. If you sometimes feel inadequate and unable to pray, to participate in discussion, or even to lead devotions, remember that each person needs to *practice devoting* to feel more confident and assured in communicating with God and with each other.

Try different seating arrangements (circular, small groups within one large group, partner-devoting, for example). Also add different dimensions for devotions from time to time. (Join hands in a circle while singing or praying, for example.)

Remember the words of the writer to the Hebrews, **"Let us draw near to God with a sincere heart in full assurance of faith. Let us not give up meeting**

together . . . but let us encourage one another" (Hebrews 10:25).

Jesus is with you.

DEVOTING PEOPLE THEN

Read the following Scripture passages. Then describe the group, the ways they devoted themselves to God, and God's response, if any, to the people.

Genesis 8:20 and **9:16** ______________________

____

____

Exodus 15:1-18 ______________________

____

____

1 Kings 8 ______________________

____

____

Daniel 3 ______________________

____

____

Luke 2:17 and **20** ______________________

____

____

Matthew 2:11 ____________________

____

____

Matthew 14:13-21 ____________________

____

____

Luke 11:1-13 ____________________

____

____

Matthew 26:17-29 ____________________

____

____

Luke 24:13-35 ____________________

____

____

Acts 2:1 and **2:42-47** ____________________

____

____

DEVOTING PEOPLE NOW

1. Jesus told Peter then, and He tells us today how to follow Him. He says in **John 13:34-35, "A new commandment I give you: Love one another. As I have loved you, so you must love one another. All men will know that you are My disciples if you love one another."** Briefly tell how you must feel about God, others, and yourself before you can devote anything to Him.

____

____

2. When you live by the Spirit, remembering you are free from sin and remembering that Christ is living IN you, what spiritual "fruit" will you experience according to **Galatians 5:22-23?**

____

3. Sometimes, following the order of service in *Lutheran Worship*, you might sing the "Offertory." We prayerfully sing these words from **Psalm 51:10-12, "Create in me a clean heart, O God, and renew a right spirit within me. Cast me not away from your presence, and take not your Holy Spirit from me. Restore to me the joy of your salvation, and uphold me with your free Spirit."** How does this Scripture passage make you feel?

____

____

4. How are we to worship, according to **Psalm 95:1-2?**

____

____

How else can we worship, according to **verse 6?**

____

5. What does Paul tell us about worship in his letter to the **Colossians 4:2-3?**

____

____

HOW DO WE BEGIN GROUP WORSHIP?

1. Paul instructed the people, in his letter to the Romans, to **"accept one another, then, just as Christ accepted you, in order to bring praise to God" (Romans 15:7).** Why do you think it's important to accept each other? ____________________

____

____

2. As you look through *Lutheran Worship*, make notes here about any parts of a worship service that you would like to personally use in group devotions. Tell why the parts you've chosen are important and meaningful to you. ____________________

____

____

____

3. Describe your favorite and most meaningful part of your class' group devotions. ____________________

____

____

____

Encourage one another and build each other up, just as in fact you are doing.

1 Thessalonians 5:11

Be filled with the Spirit. Speak to one another with psalms, hymns and spiritual songs. Sing and make music in your heart to the Lord, always giving thanks to God the Father for everything, in the name of our Lord Jesus Christ.

Ephesians 5:18-20

Session 8

We Worship (Part 1)

A sign on a church door reads, "Come in to worship. Go out to serve."

Here are some questions to think about: What does "worship" mean to you? How do you picture God or Jesus when you worship? And how do you feel when you've really worshiped?

Let's find out more about "worship" and its significance for you.

WHAT IS WORSHIP?

1. First, worship is *active*. It's something we DO. We act certain ways when we worship. Read **Psalm 95:6.** Write the verbs you read in this verse. How do we sometimes act?

____

____

a. Who "worshiped and bowed down" according to **Matthew 2:11?**

____

____

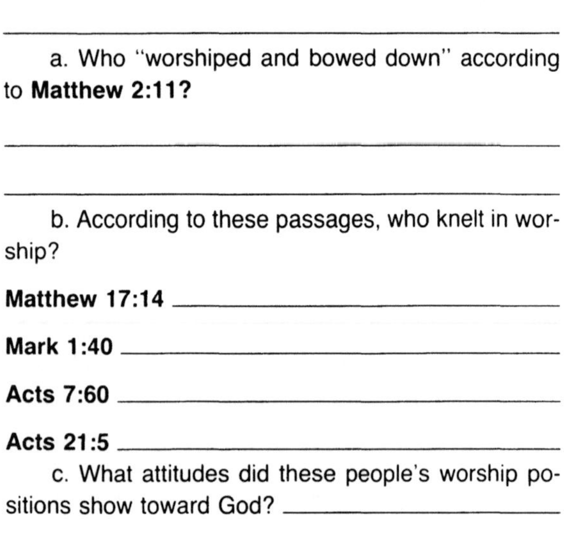

b. According to these passages, who knelt in worship?

Matthew 17:14 ______________________

Mark 1:40 ______________________

Acts 7:60 ______________________

Acts 21:5 ______________________

c. What attitudes did these people's worship positions show toward God? ______________________

____

2. Worship is also *service*. To worship means to do work. It means that we involve ourselves in giving all that we are and have to serve and glorify God.

a. Tell how these passages describe worship as work.

Joshua 24:14-24 ______________________

Hebrews 9:14 ______________________

Hebrews 12:28 ______________________

b. How does **Romans 12:1** help you understand the idea of worship? What do you think it means to "offer your bodies as living sacrifices to God"?

____

c. What are some ways you can encourage each other to worship? ______________________

____

d. How does being assured of and receiving God's forgiveness through Christ Jesus help you worship?

____

3. We can say these three things about worship:

a. **Worship begins with God.** We Christians always worship because of Christ! Tell what **Ephesians 1:12** says about our worship. ______________________

____

b. **Worship centers on what God has done for us through His Son, Jesus Christ.** We worship God because He fulfilled the promise to His Old Testament people by sending Jesus, and at the same time, made a new promise with us, His New Testament people, through Jesus' blood. **John 3:16** reminds us of God's love in action.

c. **Worship centers on the Holy Spirit, too.** We worship God because He continuously cares for us and sends us His Spirit to keep us in the faith. Through Jesus' death and resurrection, God gives us victory over death. Through worship, we celebrate Christ's triumph over death, the hope He gives us for eternal life, and the fellowship the Spirit gives us with God and all believers.

WORSHIP THROUGH GOD'S WORD

1. Most of the church's liturgy is taken from Scripture. Look at Divine Service II (First Setting) in *Lutheran Worship*.

Tell in what part of the worship setting you find:

1 John 1:8-9 ______________________

Psalm 116:12-13, 18-19 ______________________

2. Why is it important that Scripture gives "body" to the liturgy in our worship? ______________________

____

3. Find the place in the worship service for the *Introit*. From which book in Scripture is the *Introit* taken?

____

A choir or the congregation might sing the *Introit* for the day, or the congregation might sing an entrance hymn. This Word of God begins the worship service.

4. What Word of God follows the *Collect*?

____

5. The *Gradual for the Season* or the appointed *Psalm* is then sung or said. This custom of responding to God's Word by singing or saying parts of psalms is an ancient one.

6. What Word of God follows the *Gradual*?

____

This Scripture reading, usually from a New Testament letter, tells us how to practice and live the Good News of our salvation in our daily lives.

7. After the choir or congregation sings a *Verse*, what is the third reading from Scripture?

____

The pastor reads from one of the first four New Testament Gospels, describing for us the life of Jesus and His Words to the people before He went into heaven.

8. God "called" your pastor to preach God's Word to you and to the members of your congregation. Much like the Old Testament prophets, your pastor tells you God's Word and helps make it meaningful to your daily life. We believe that as the pastor speaks to us, God Himself talks to us! Your pastor preaches God's message **(2 Corinthians 4:5-7)** to Christians in your congregation **(2 Corinthians 4:13-15)** for all the people to hear **(Ephesians 3:8-10).**

LITURGY IN WORSHIP

1. Read **1 Thessalonians 2:13.** According to this verse, the Word of God is active. Tell what God's Word does in and for you. ______________________

____

In a worship setting, God's Word enlightens the *liturgy*, the formal words we follow. At the same time, those formal words of the liturgy proclaim—through the pastors and the "liturgists"—the Word of God! So, the liturgy then is the "shared worship" in which we all participate. Through this liturgy, you and the people around you actively worship God. You show your worship by DOING your worshiping. Your whole self and all your senses become involved. When you worship, you might feel emotionally moved, as though your soul is stirred!

2. Describe in a few words how you honestly feel when you walk into a worship service. ______________________

____

Do you feel more comfortable with a few friends in a group devotion or with many people in a church worship setting?

Do you enjoy worship with formality and liturgy, or do you prefer a more informal worship?

When you worship, do you feel fellowship and a sense of "family" with the people around you?

How do you usually feel after you have worshiped?

3. The word "liturgy" means "the work of the people." It IS work to concentrate on what is happening in the worship service, to listen intently to the readings of Scripture, to hear and be able to apply the pastor's sermon message to your life, and to honestly and wholeheartedly worship. Worship takes your effort. By working at worshiping, your Lord and Savior will draw you closer to Himself.

Worship the Lord in the splendor of His holiness.
1 Chronicles 16:29

Session 9

We Worship (Part 2)

Let's pretend.

It's possible for you to give ANYONE a gift. The gift can be ANYTHING you choose. Whatever you wish will come true.

Describe your recipient and the gift you would give to him or her.

Be prepared to share your gift-giving fantasy with your class.

God presents us with special gifts when we worship Him. These gifts are a way for God to give us His grace. They are "sacramental" and full of His love and grace. These gifts are better than any imaginable gift in the whole world! In His gift-giving, God comes down to us and blesses us through His Word, through the Sacrament of Holy Baptism, and through the Sacrament of Holy Communion. Let's find out more about each of these gifts in worship. Let's discover what's IN God's gifts to and for us.

GOD'S GIFT—HIS HOLY WORD

1. You've probably received a book as a birthday or a Christmas gift. Write its title and a short description here.

2. God's Word, the Holy Bible, contains God's own words to us. Tell why the Bible is different from any book you've ever received as a gift.

3. Tell in your own words what Paul writes about God's Word to the Thessalonians in **1 Thessalonians 2:13.**

4. According to these passages, tell why God gave us His Word:

2 Timothy 3:15-17

Psalm 119:105

5. List some of the places from *Lutheran Worship*—Divine Service II—where we use God's Word in our worship.

6. Why is it important for us to hear, read, and learn God's Word and use it in worship?

GOD'S GIFT—THE SACRAMENT OF BAPTISM

You probably learned from studying the catechism that God Himself instituted Baptism, because it was Jesus who commanded us all to **"go and make disciples of all nations, baptizing them in the name of the Father and of the Son and of the Holy Spirit" (Matthew 28:19).**

1. What blessings does God give us in His gift of Baptism?

Acts 22:16 ________________

Romans 6:3-4 ________________

1 Peter 3:21 ________________

God's Word gives these blessings to Baptism. Through faith we accept God's forgiveness and salvation He offers us in Baptism. He makes these blessings ours.

Baptism is a one-time promise, but we need to live our baptisms each day. We aren't physically baptized more than once with the Word and the water by the pastor at the baptismal font in the church. But we receive the benefits of Baptism every day! By confessing our sins and by believing God erases those sins, we continually become "new creatures" and forgiven sinner-saints.

2. Tell what **Romans 6:3-5** means to you. ______

3. You might read to yourself the service of *Holy Baptism* from *Lutheran Worship* pages 199-204.

GOD'S GIFT—THE SACRAMENT OF HOLY COMMUNION

1. God comes to us through the Sacrament of Holy Communion. What are some other names for this sacrament?

2. What is Holy Communion? **(Matthew 26:26-28)**?

3. When we share in the eating and drinking of Jesus' body and blood, we obey His command, **"This do in remembrance of Me" (Luke 22:19).**

According to these passages, why do we need Holy Communion?

2 Corinthians 5:15, 17 ________________

Luke 22:19, 20 ________________

Acts 2:42 ________________

We receive God's gift of forgiveness through Holy Communion by believing the words, "Given and shed for you for the remission of sins."

4. Read to yourself the preparation for Holy Communion, the Communion liturgy, and Post-Communion liturgy from *Lutheran Worship* pages 170-175.

5. Describe the specific words, prayers, and/or songs that are especially meaningful for you in worship and tell why.

A prayer to pray today: *Dear God, we thank you for all the blessings we receive from Your Word and from the Sacraments of Baptism and Holy Communion. Give us the strength and power to confess our sins and live new, forgiven lives each day, in Jesus' name. Amen.*

Praise be to the God and Father of our Lord Jesus Christ, who has blessed us in the heavenly realms with every spiritual blessing in Christ.

Ephesians 1:3

Session 10

We Worship (Part 3)

Two men went to the temple to pray.

One man, the Pharisee, prayed proudly, loudly, and boastingly, "Thanks, God, for making me so good! I'm not as sinful as robbers, adulterers, and cheaters. I'm glad I'm not as bad as that tax collector over there! I keep ALL the rules. I fast twice a week, and I give a tenth of everything I get to the poor people."

The tax collector stood in a corner of the temple by himself.

He prayed humbly, with his head bowed lowly, and hit his own chest crying, "Oh, God, please forgive me. I'm a sinner. Have mercy, Oh, God." Jesus told this story recorded in **Luke 18:9-14.**

Prayer is an important part of our worship. When we pray, we "sacrifice" our thoughts, our feelings and emotions, and our words to God. We offer them all to God. Which man truly sacrificed through his prayer in the temple?

You'll learn more about your own sacrificial worship acts in this session.

OLD TESTAMENT SACRIFICIAL ACTS OF WORSHIP

Read the following passages. Then describe the worshipers and the nature of their sacrifices.

Genesis 8:20-21 ______________________

____

1 Samuel 1:11 ______________________

____

Deuteronomy 26:1-15 ______________________

____

Ezra 10:1-17 ______________________

____

Draw coins and fruit and grain beside the Scripture referring to "tithes and first fruits" offerings.

Draw raindrops beside the reference to people who dedicatedly confessed their sins in heavy rain.

Draw an animal next to the reference of people sacrificing animal offerings and prayers to God.

Draw a heart beside the passage that refers to someone offering a promise to God.

CHRIST—THE NEW TESTAMENT SACRIFICE FOR ALL PEOPLE

1. Read **Hebrews 9:1—10:25.** Why is Christ called a "high priest"?

____

2. What does Christ, our High Priest, offer **(9:14)?**

____

____

3. What does Christ make sure for us through His offering **(9:15)**?

____

4. Read **Hebrews 10:5-7.** Tell why Christ's words are important to you.

____

5. Read the words of the *Hymns of Praise* from *Lutheran Worship* pages 160-163. What feelings do you have when you read the hymns' words?

____

____

OUR SACRIFICIAL ACTS IN WORSHIP

1. Read these Scripture passages and find out

ways that people in the New Testament offered their praise, thanks, and themselves to God: **Matthew 9:8; Luke 7:16; Acts 2:47; Acts 3:8.**

2. Discover from these passages the importance of offering to God material things: **2 Corinthians 8:1-12; 9:1-15; Hebrews 13:16.**

3. We respond to God's love and forgiveness in certain acts of worship. Look at the following parts of worship from *Lutheran Worship* (pages 158-177) and tell what your action, your "offering to God," is in each part.

a. *The Introit, Psalm or Entrance Hymn*

____

____

b. *The Kyrie*

____

____

c. *The Hymn of Praise and The Hymn of the Day*

____

____

d. *The Creed*

____

____

e. *The Prayers*

____

____

f. *The Offering*

____

____

MY SACRIFICE IN WORSHIP

As a believer in Christ, your Savior, you respond in your own unique way during worship. God comes to you through His Word and in the Sacraments. You, then, DO your personal worship and actively show God your devotion to Him.

1. According to **Romans 12:1-2,** what should be your sacrifice? ____________________

2. What should your attitude be toward your offerings to God, according to **2 Corinthians 8:5?**

____

____

3. Describe yourself as the writer does in **1 Peter 2:4-10.**

____

____

4. Which is personally easier for you to "sacrifice"—(a) prayers, praise, and thanks to God through your words, or (b) offerings of substance such as money? Why?

____

____

How do you feel about one offering being more important than another? ____________________

Tell in your own words what **1 Chronicles 29:14** says about substance offerings. ____________________

____

5. Why is *The Creed* a sacrifice? ____________________

____

Write your own Christian creed. Then share it with a friend. Be prepared to also share your creed with your class.

____

____

____

____

____

____

____

6. Pray today, using one of the *Offertories* from *Lutheran Worship* pages 168 and 169.

May my prayer be set before You like incense; may the lifting up of my hands be like the evening sacrifice.

Psalm 141:2

. . . I urge you . . . in view of God's mercy, to offer your bodies as living sacrifices, holy and pleasing to God—which is your spiritual worship.

Romans 12:1

Through Jesus, therefore, let us continually offer to God a sacrifice of praise—the fruit of lips that confess His name.

Hebrews 13:15

Session 11

Concluding Activities for Unit 2

Choose a worship project from the following list. If you have a different idea for a worship project, ask your teacher to approve it. Aim to personalize worship and make your project meaningful for you and for those with whom you will share it.

1. Keep a personal spiritual journal for at least two weeks. In a diary or on a calendar, write your thoughts, feelings, and ideas for your own worship life. You might read *How to Keep a Spiritual Journal* by Ronald Klug (Thomas Nelson Publishers, N.Y., 1982). Check if it's in your library. The author gives helpful and interesting ways to keep a spiritual journal as well as personal excerpts from his own journal. Then tell your classmates how keeping a personal journal helped you in your own devotional life.

2. Write a set of three personal devotions based on three different parables from Scripture. Share these printed devotions with your classmates for their personal use. Tell why you chose certain parables and give reasons for your themes.

3. Write one devotion that could be used by a group. Choose a meaningful theme. Share this printed devotion with your class. Be prepared to lead part or all of it during a class session.

4. Write an original song (lyrics and/or music) of praise, thanksgiving, or supplication. Share it with your class. You might ask a musician friend to help you.

5. Paraphrase a psalm from Scripture. Set it to original music. You might also use choreography with the psalm's words to create a "psalm-dance." Be prepared to present it alone, or with a group of friends, to your class.

6. Write two morning and two evening devotions that you could use with a family or a group of families on a campout or retreat. Share these printed devotions with class members. Explain your themes and activities.

7. Decide on a very special, meaningful way you can "offer yourself" and your services to someone. Pray about this project and do it in a BIG, CELEBRATING way! Then write a project report. Tell how you served and the results of your service. (Remember that you might see few results immediately; the Holy Spirit works in and through people long after you serve, and you might never see or know the long-range results.)

GOD'S PEACE AND BLESSING IN YOUR WORSHIP!

Unit 3

Growing in My Relationships with Others

It's easy for some people to choose friends, but this seems like an almost impossible task for others. Some people are too shy and withdrawn. Others are outgoing and talkative. Some are easily offended by almost everything. Others are able to "roll with the punches." Some have ethical and moral standards that are true to Scripture and are like your own. Others find it easy to bend the truth, to not give Mom all the change, or to "pocket" an article from a store now and then.

All of us, young and old alike, face the big questions, "Whom do I want for friends?" "What really is a friend?" "How can I build lasting friendships?" "What causes friendships to fall apart, and what can I do to restore them?"

In this series of lessons we will look for answers to those questions.

Session 12

Friends—Pick and Choose One or More Friends.

Who's your best friend?

Is it God? You've talked a lot about your relationship with God so far in this course. God really is your friend. Maybe you would like to give God another name: My Best Friend.

But what about other people? Do you have a "best friend" in your school? at church? among the other kids you know? at home? What do you like about this "best friend"?

______

______

______

GOD WANTS US TO HAVE FRIENDS

1. After God created the first person, Adam, He said, **"It is not good for the man to be alone. I will make a helper suitable for him" (Genesis 2:18).** Since God did not find a helper among the things He had already created, He now created one. Whom did God now create **(verses 21-22)**?

______

2. You probably know about the friendship of David and Jonathan **(1 Samuel 18:1-4; 19:1-7; 20:1-42; 2 Samuel 1:17-27; 9:1-13).** According to **1 Samuel 19:4**, how did Jonathan "live" his friendship?

______

3. The friendship continued even after Jonathan died. What did David do for Jonathan's crippled son, Mephibosheth **(2 Samuel 9:10)**?

______

4. Sometimes you might feel like you don't have a friend in the whole world. Elijah felt something like that **(1 Kings 19:1-18).** It seemed to him that everyone had refused to listen to his message and was worshiping an idol, Baal. What did God tell Elijah **(verse 18)**?

______

5. What are friends for? What does God tell us in these verses?

Proverbs 17:17 ______

Ecclesiastes 4:10 ______

John 15:12-13 ______

6. Do your friends ever let you down? And then do you feel (as did Elijah) that you don't have a friend in the whole world? Copy some words from **Hebrews 13:5** that will help you at times like that.

______

PICKING FRIENDS

You've probably asked yourself the question, "Whom should I choose for friends, and why?"

1. Stop a minute and think of the last person you tried to befriend. Why did you want to have that person for a friend? ______

______

2. Is everyone that you know *really* your friend? ______ If not, why not?

______

______

3. There are different levels, or degrees, of friendships. Identify some of them.

a. ______

b. ______

c. ______

d. ______

e. ___

f. ___

4. Are all friends about the same age as you? Or is there an older person or two whom you think of as your friend? If so, tell about them. ___

___

___

___

5. Are there any people whom you do not want as friends? If so, what types of people are they, and why wouldn't you want them as friends?

___

6. Write a reaction to this statement: "Cliques" aren't always bad.

___

___

___

7. Are parents ever your friends? Could they be your friends? What do you think it would take to make parents your friends? Answer these questions on a separate sheet of paper.

8. Could your pastor or one of your teachers ever be your friend? If so, how? Write a paragraph answering this, also.

It's not easy to pick friends and build friendships. It takes time to find the right kind of friends, and to develop lasting friendships. But good friends and friendships are well worth the effort. Why don't you see how many good friends and friendships you can develop during this school year?

As you do this, remember that friends are gifts from God. We have very few *true* friends in a lifetime, and HE is the best Friend we will ever have. He will help you find friends who will stand by you in good times and in bad.

A SPECIAL PROJECT

Think of an activity or event that can help to build friendships. Then try to establish it in your school. (Be sure to first discuss the possible activity or event with your instructor.)

The Lord God said, "It is not good for the man to be alone. I will make a helper suitable for him."

Genesis 2:18

A friend loves at all times, and a brother is born for adversity.

Proverbs 17:17

If one falls down, a friend can help him up.

Ecclesiastes 4:10

"My command is this: Love each other as I have loved you. Greater love has no one that this, that one lay down his life for his friends."

John 15:12-13

I urge you, brothers, to watch out for those who cause divisions and put obstacles in your way that are contrary to the teaching you have learned. Keep away from them.

Romans 16:17

Session 13

Building Friendships

In our last lesson we talked about choosing the right friends. Today we want to think about ways that would help friendships grow closer together.

We need to learn and develop skills for building friendships with other people. It usually doesn't just happen.

Our lesson today points out certain critical areas in building friendships. Perhaps you can add areas that will help to build even better friendships.

"FRIENDSHIP WORDS"

1. Check the words below that describe characteristics that will help to build friendships.

a. Humility ______ f. Conceit __________
b. Anger________ g. Compassion ______
c. Kindness ______ h. Encouragement ____
d. Patience ______ i. Faithfulness _______
e. Selfishness ____ j. Rivalry ___________

2. After reading the following passages from Scripture, write a word that describes the main emphasis of each passage:

a. **Hebrews 10:24-25** ______________

b. **Matthew 25:14-30** ______________

c. **James 5:7-9** ______________

d. **Ruth 3:10** ______________

e. **Luke 10:30-37** ______________

f. **Luke 14:7-11** ______________

3. Check your answers for the above questions. How are they the same? If there are differences, what are they? Why?

____
____
____
____
____
____
____

4. List appropriate synonyms for the answers for #2.

____
____
____
____
____

5. What other major areas in building friendships might have been overlooked, and should be included in our list of friendship-building qualities?

____
____

LIVING IN FRIENDSHIP

1. Give some everyday examples of how you can "live" each of the words from #2 above.

____
____
____
____
____
____
____
____
____
____
____
____

The **Book of Ruth** (especially chapters 1—3) describes the friendship between Ruth and her mother-in-law, Naomi. God lived in both of these women and led them to do some very loving things for each other. A very close friendship developed.

2. What were some things Ruth did for Naomi?

3. What were some things Naomi did for Ruth?

4. Write a paragraph about a friend. Include some thoughts about the following: How did you become friends? What is your friend like? What are some things you both like to do? What are some things one of you likes to do, but the other doesn't? How do you show love and respect for each other (for example, when you want to do different things)?

Building friendships takes both time and effort. But it is worth it! Ask God to bless the time and effort you use to build friendships, to keep you from not only being alone, but also lonely. Take the time and the effort, and work at building friendships. Some friendships you will develop now will not only last all your life, but they will enrich your life over and over.

Therefore, as God's chosen people, holy and dearly loved, clothe yourselves with compassion, kindness, humility, gentleness, and patience.

Colossians 3:13

Be faithful, even to the point of death, and I will give you the crown of life.

Revelation 2:10

And let us consider how we may spur one another on toward love and good deeds.

Hebrews 10:24

Session 14

Destroying Friendships (Part 1)

"I really thought he was my friend. But yesterday when we were talking, I said something he didn't like, and he started raising his voice, and the next thing I knew, he stomped off in a huff. I'm not even sure why he is angry, so I hardly know how to talk to him. Maybe if I wait a few days, he will calm down and we can discuss the situation calmly. I sure hope so! I want him to be my friend, but I'm not sure, now that this has happened, that he wants to be mine."

HOW SIN AFFECTS FRIENDSHIPS

1. After God created Adam and Eve, they lived as His perfect friends and as perfect friends to each other. Imagine what life must have been like in the Garden of Eden. Surely Adam and Eve did not try to hide any secrets from each other—or from God! And God did not keep secrets from them.

But Adam and Eve sinned. How did sin affect friendships in the following verses in **Genesis?**

3:8 ______________________

3:12 ______________________

4:8 ______________________

37:8 ______________________

37:28 ______________________

2. Things have not changed much. Sin still causes problems among friends. Give some examples.

____

____

____

____

3. Fortunately, our loving God gives us a way to deal with sin. First of all, He forgives the sins of all who believe in Him. Secondly, He gives us the power to forgive those who sin against us. How did forgiveness affect the friendships of Joseph and his brothers **(Genesis 50:15-21)?**

____

____

____

____

ANGER

1. Recall as many things as you can that make you angry—things that really irritate you. Have someone write these on the board. Do some of these "irritants" fall into groups? If so, group them.

2. Talk about things you notice about your list. For example, does not having things done "your way" be-

come a major "irritant" and make you angry? What relationship, if any, do you notice between egotism and anger?

3. Read **Matthew 5:21-24.** Think carefully about what it says. Then read **Ephesians 4:26-27.** Now answer the following questions:

a. Why do you think Jesus spoke of judgment in connection with both anger and murder?

____

____

b. What does "Raca" mean?

____

c. Have you ever called anyone a fool? If so, are you going to spend eternity in hell? What did Jesus mean by His words in **Matthew 5:22**?

____

____

d. Explain verses **23 and 24.**

____

____

e. How is it possible for a person to be angry and yet not sin **(Ephesians 4:26)?**

____

____

f. How soon should you try to make peace with the person you are angry with?

____

4. Some people say that anger is an uncontrollable emotion. What do you think? Talk about it. What insights do **Genesis 44:18, Psalm 37:8,** and **Ecclesiastes 7:9** give to this topic?

DEALING WITH ANGER

1. What does God advise us to do when anger begins to grow **(Proverbs 15:1; 19:11)**?

____

2. Usually we sin when we get angry. We think sinful thoughts and we do sinful things as a result of our anger. What directions and good news do you find for such a time in **1 John 1:9?**

____

____

3. How do you think it will affect a friendship if one of the friends confesses to the other that he or she was angry with the other person?

____

____

4. What should you do when you really feel like being angry? If you withhold your anger, some serious side effects may grow within you. You may become emotionally depressed—feel sad and sort of numb, develop an "I don't care" attitude, and experience an inability to get your work done. Serious physical, mental, emotional, and social problems can follow. So what should you do? Which of the following do you think would be good ways to cope with your anger? Check all that apply.

____ a. Say things in anger.
____ b. Pound a pillow, go for a run, or work out in the gym until you are "cooled off."
____ c. Go to the person and confront him or her with the issue and try to talk it out to a satisfactory conclusion.
____ d. Talk about the problem with your parents or a teacher.
____ e. Get into a fight with the person.
____ f. Pray for strength and guidance.
____ g. Other. (List your own idea.)

____

____

Now rank the ideas you checked. Put a 1 in front of the best thing to do, a 2 by the next best, etc.

A gentle answer turns away wrath, but a harsh word stirs up anger.

Proverbs 15:1

A man's wisdom gives him patience; it is to his glory to overlook an offense.

Proverbs 19:11

In your anger do not sin. Do not let the sun go down while you are still angry.

Ephesians 4:26

Session 15

Destroying Friendships (Part 2)

THE BEGINNING OF SIN

In the last session we saw how sin caused friendships to be destroyed. Here is one version of the first sin:

"Hi, Eve! My name is Sam Serpent, your friendly fruit distributor. I specialize in knowing all the different kinds and types of fruit available in the world today. I know almost all of them, but there's this one that I'm not too sure about. It's the fruit in the middle of your garden. Can you tell me anything about it?"

"Why, yes I can," replied Eve. "God told us to enjoy all the fruit in the garden except the fruit from the tree in the middle of the garden."

"What? Why would God say a thing like that? Are you sure God really told you not to eat that fruit? What's up? Is it some kind of rare fruit already on the verge of extinction? That's hard to believe, since the world was just created!"

"I'm sure I'm right. God told us not to eat the fruit from that tree, or even touch it, because if we did, we would die."

"Die? Die? What does that mean? Listen to me, Eve. You won't die. Instead, your eyes will be opened, and you will be like God. You don't know it, but God is holding out on you. Right now you only know good. But when you eat of the fruit, you will know both good and evil. You'll be just like God!"

"Just like God?" Eve thought to herself. "Wow, would that be neat! Then I wouldn't have to take orders from God. Instead, God and I could sit down and talk to each other as equals. That's it! Equals! God and I would be equal—and I would know just as much as He does. This sounds like a pretty good deal. Equal to God. What could be better?"

So Eve looked at the fruit and it looked absolutely delicious. She ate some, and since she loved Adam very much, she gave some to him and he ate.

In the beginning, God and people were at peace with one another and enjoyed a happy, harmonious relationship. What kinds of feelings, or attitudes, led to the destruction of that relationship? Underline the word or words below that describe those feelings—the feelings that you think destroyed that beautiful relationship.

Pride
Conceit
Self-esteem
Arrogance
Egotism
Rebellion

PRIDE AND REBELLION

1. Read the following paragraph, and then discuss it in class.

How can humans be filled with feelings of both inadequacy and arrogance? Are humans both proud and humble at the same time, or do they switch back and forth whenever other people give them either compliments or criticisms? Is it possible to become so humble that you become proud of your humility? Can people become so humble that God cannot use them as He wishes? How do you find the proper balance between *pride* and *humility*? What do **Proverbs 3:34** and **1 Peter 5:5-6** say about these two words?

2. Briefly review the story of Absalom's conspiracy and tragic end **(2 Samuel 15 and 18).** Then answer these questions:

a. What was the root of Absalom's problem?

____

b. How did David feel about the situation?

____

c. What were David's orders to his army?

____

d. What did David do after he learned of Absalom's death? Why? ______________________

____

e. Explain the relationship of David to Absalom and God to us. ______________________

____

f. How does God resolve our problems?

---

g. What is the relationship between pride and rebellion?

---

3. Most teenagers rebel against authority—often. On a separate piece of paper write the last three rebellious acts against authority that you can recall. Now bow your head and pray to God to forgive you for acting in a rebellious way. Then take the piece of paper, tear it in tiny pieces, and deposit it in the waste basket on your way out of the class. Just as you threw the paper away, God has taken away all your sins.

4. Read **2 Chronicles 26:3-5 and 16-21.** God certainly did not treat pride and rebellion lightly in this instance. Do you think the punishment fit the crime, or was God too severe on Uzziah? Talk about it.

5. How much time each day do you spend on your personal appearance? How much time each day do you spend thinking about clothes, hair styles, make-up, etc? Does God want us to be sloppy and dirty? Does God want us to replace Him with a private ego-trip? Read God's advice to all of us, as found in **Matthew 6:25-34.** Describe a God-pleasing attitude toward personal appearance.

THE BATTLE WITHIN ME

Walking the tight-rope between self-acceptance (feeling good about yourself because God made you and forgave your sins) and pride (feeling arrogant, egotistical, and even rebellious because you feel *too* good about yourself) is a tight-rope act that will last all your life. No matter how hard you try to feel differently, at times you will feel worthless, and at other times you will feel smug, cocky, and in control.

When success comes your way, give God the glory because He deserves it. When defeat or tragedy comes your way, look for a way God can turn this event into a blessing. At the very least, you can thank God for keeping you *truly* humble. As Paul says in **Philippians 4:4, "Rejoice in the Lord always. I will say it again: Rejoice!"**

Young men, in the same way be submissive to those who are older. Clothe yourselves with humility toward one another, because "God opposes the proud but gives grace to the humble." Humble yourselves, therefore, under God's mighty hand, that He may lift you up in due time.

1 Peter 5:5-6

Seek first His kingdom and His righteousness, and all these things will be given to you as well.

Matthew 6:33

Session 16

Restoring Friendships

Once a friendship has been ruined, it will probably be harder to restore it to its original relationship than it was to build it in the first place.

We like to say, "Forgive and forget." All too often, however, it is hard to undo the damage that has been done. This is particularly true if the cause of the fractured friendship hurt deeply. Because we are both saint and sinner, our "saint self" forgives, but our "sinner self" remembers the hurt.

POWER TO FORGIVE

Probably no other act can work so powerfully to restore a broken friendship as the act of forgiving a friend—and telling him or her about the forgiveness. But how can we forgive someone who has hurt us? Where do we get the power to forgive?

1. Read **2 Corinthians 5:11-21.** Some people apparently didn't think Paul should have been bringing the Gospel to certain "lower class" people or "sinners." Copy words from the following verses that tell why Paul was moved to love and forgive those people.

5:14 ______________________________

5:15 ______________________________

5:17 ______________________________

5:21 ______________________________

2. Now read **Ephesians 4:31-32.** Here Paul is speaking of problems in relationships among Christians—the kinds of problems we have been talking about. How do we get the power to be forgiving to each other?

____

3. Summarize what you have learned in these passages. Why are we able to be loving and forgiving to others?

____

RESTORING BROKEN FRIENDSHIPS

Scripture mentions certain qualities and techniques that can help us rebuild fractured friendships. Perhaps you are wrestling right now with a broken friendship that you would like to see restored. As you work through this lesson, try to apply these techniques and qualities to your problem. They may be just the things you are looking for.

1. The following Bible passages contain some basic qualities that one needs to possess if broken friendships are to be restored. Copy the references on a separate sheet of paper. After each one:

—write down one word that you think best describes the quality described (a quality needed to restore friendships), and

—write a sentence or two telling why you think such a quality would be helpful.

a. **1 Peter 5:6**
b. **James 5:16**
c. **1 John 1:9**
d. **Leviticus 19:18**
e. **1 Peter 2:20**
f. **Ephesians 4:32**
g. **Proverbs 11:13**
h. **James 3:18**
i. **2 Peter 1:6**
j. **2 Samuel 12:1-13**
k. **Luke 15:20**
l. **1 Thessalonians 5:17**

2. **What if . . .** Discuss the following questions in class. Try to find Scripture references that apply as you answer the questions.

a. What if you feel that you just can't forgive the other person?

b. What if you really can't pray about it because you're still so angry, or hurt?

c. What if you really don't want to restore the broken friendship?

d. What if your parents and you are no longer "friends" because *they* wronged *you*?

e. What if you feel that the person you'd like to be friends with again just can't be trusted?

f. What if the other person insists on dominating you in the friendship, and you broke off once before over this same issue?

g. What if you broke off your friendship because the other person wanted you to join him or her in bad habits (drugs, alcohol, etc.), and now the other person is coming to you and wants to be a friend again?

3. Suppose you and your parents are not speaking to one another because you challenged their authority, and they have "grounded" you. What should you do? Would it be better to show them you have opinions and ideas that need to be heard, and hold your ground, or would it be better to give in to their authority? Which position do you think will bring you more freedom and responsibility sooner? Why? Look at the qualities you listed for #1 above. Which of those qualities would be especially useful for you in this situation? Why? (You might wish that your parents showed more of those qualities in this situation, too. Remember, though, that in restoring friendships you need to focus upon the things YOU can do. Usually we have little control over the things other people do.)

A FINAL WORD

Restoring broken friendships usually includes a lot of "giving" and very little "taking." If both parties give a lot, the friendship will probably be restored. But if one person wants to prove who was "right" in the first place, the friendship will probably remain broken.

So what's the secret to restoring friendships? First of all, we can't restore them on our own. God's Spirit needs to live within us; He will fill us with the qualities we need. And God has to bless our efforts in order for them to succeed. He usually does this as we seek to live in ways that demonstrate qualities like love, forgiveness, and humility. Finally, steps toward restoration go in both directions, and we can only control one direction; but the steps we take toward reconciliation usually affect the other person in a way that will cause conciliatory steps to walk our way, too.

Confess your sin to each other and pray for each other so that you may be healed. The prayer of a righteous man is powerful and effective.

James 5:16

The fruit of the Spirit is love, joy, peace, patience, kindness, goodness, faithfulness, gentleness and self-control. Against such things there is no law.

Galatians 5:22-23

You will keep in perfect peace him whose mind is steadfast, because he trusts in you.

Isaiah 26:3

Session 17

Peer Pressure

How do you decide what kinds of clothes to buy for school? How often do you ask yourself, "What is everyone else wearing? If I don't dress like the other kids, will they still accept me, or will they make fun of me instead?" Do you think you should "give in" to pressure about clothes? How do you decide?

Or think of the ninth grade girl who said, "Most of the kids I run around with smoke. They keep asking me to join them. I really don't want to smoke, because I know it's bad for my health, but I don't want to lose their friendships. What should I do?"

Psychological studies done on "peer pressure" have shown that three out of four people (75%) want to be accepted so much by their peers that they will agree that "green is white" if all the others agree that "green is white," even though they know full well that "green is green."

All of us live with peer pressure all of our lives. It's not easy to be the "only one" in a situation—in fact, it's very difficult.

As you study the concept of "peer pressure," be as honest as possible with yourself. But remember, sometimes it won't be easy!

CONVICTION OR PEER PRESSURE?

1. Circle the answers to the following questions:

a. I you would rather go to a symphony concert than a rock concert. yes no

b. I would rather go to church than to a movie. yes no

c. I hope to own my own car someday. yes no

d. I think it would be improper for me to kiss a person of the opposite sex in a passionate way before I'm engaged to that person. yes no

e. I enjoy being laughed at by the rest of the crowd because I didn't "go along" with something. yes no

f. I believe I am a sinner, but am forgiven through the blood of Jesus Christ. yes no

During class compare your answers with your classmates' answers. On which question or questions did you feel most comfortable? most uneasy? Why?

2. Look carefully at yourself and see what kind of clothes you are wearing. Are you dressed like most of the other students in this room? If you are, could it be that you are submitting to peer pressure without even knowing it? Is all peer pressure "bad"? If not, when could it be good? Talk about it.

PEER PRESSURE IN BIBLE TIMES

1. Read the Scripture passages below. What did peer pressure cause someone to do in each passage?

John 18:15-27 ______________________________

____

Galatians 2:11-14 ______________________________

____

Matthew 27:20 ______________________________

____

Mark 15:9-15 ______________________________

____

2. Now read these passages. How did someone in each instance resist peer pressure? What did the person do?

Matthew 26:55-56 and **John 19:26-27** ______________

____

Acts 4:13-22 ______________________________

____

John 9:13-16 and **24-34** ______________________

____

3. Why were these people able to stand up against peer pressure? Peter's words in **Acts 4:8-12** give us a clue. Where did Peter get this power? ______________

____

____

4. Four of the references above mention Peter. How could someone who really "blew it" at times still

be one of Jesus' disciples and a leader in the early Christian church?

____

____

5. How about you? What parts of your relationship with God mean the most to you as you think about challenges, successes, and failures in your peer relationships?

____

____

PEER PRESSURE TODAY

1. Do you feel any peer pressure when you attend church, the youth group at church, or school? If you do, what kind of peer pressure is it? ______________

____

2. When Jesus performed miracles, lots of people started to follow Him. Some of them were just "following the crowd," so Jesus told them that He wanted more. He wanted total commitment **(Matthew 8:18-22** and **Luke 14:25-35).** What do these verses suggest about the life of a Christian today?

____

____

3. Who exerts more influence on your life—your peers or your parents? If you *really* are in trouble and need some real help, who will you turn to—your peers or your parents? On a separate sheet of paper write a paragraph in which you tell how you can have good relationships with both groups—your peers and your parents.

While it is true that we all want and need friends, we must constantly be on our guard against being led into sin or sinful habits because we want friends. If you begin to notice things going "downhill," find yourself a different group of friends. And don't forget your parents! They probably are some of the best friends you will ever have. Above all, don't forget Jesus. He will never forsake you. Remember His promise: **"Surely I will be with you always" (Matthew 28:20).**

Do not be afraid of those who kill the body but cannot kill the soul. Rather, be afraid of the one who can destroy both soul and body in hell.

Matthew 10:28

Do not conform any longer to the pattern of this world, but be transformed by the renewing of your mind. Then you will be able to test and approve what God's will is—His good, pleasing and perfect will.

Romans 12:2

Session 18

Concluding Activities for Unit 3

STRENGTH BOMBARDMENT

You are special to God. Each of your classmates is special to God. Each of you is unique. God has blessed each of you with a special personality and special gifts.

How often do you take the time to tell your classmates about some of the things that make them special?This activity will give you a chance to do this.

Ask your teacher to help you form groups of three to ten students. Maybe each group can move your chairs or desks into a small circle. Following are the directions for strength bombardment:

1. Each person should bring a blank sheet of paper or large index card to the circle. Write your name at the top of the sheet or card.

2. Pass the paper or card to the person on your left.

3. That person should write one or two things about you. The person should look for your strengths and tell about them in a few words. (You will need to decide in advance how many things to write on each sheet or card.)

4. Pass the paper or card to the person on the left again.

5. That person now should write about a strength (or strengths) of the person whose name is at the top.

6. Continue passing to the left and writing about strengths until everyone in the group has written about everyone else.

7. When you get your own sheet or card back, do one or more of the following:

a. Read the entire list of strengths silently.

b. Pray silently for a couple minutes. Thank God for the strengths He has given you and for the friends who are helping you see your strengths. Ask Him to help you use those strengths for Him and for other people in a spirit of humility.

c. Take turns in your group, telling each person some of the things you like about him or her.

d. Take turns in your group, telling one way you plan to use one of your strengths to the glory of God and the welfare of other people.

ESSAY

Write one short paragraph about each session in this unit. In three or four sentences tell about the most important part(s) of the session.

Unit 4

My Relationships with the Other Sex

"Wow! He asked me for a date! But what if I can't think of anything to talk about? I hope I don't bore him."

"I think she's getting pretty serious. I don't know if I'm ready for all that stuff yet. I don't even want to think about marriage until I'm lots older."

"I hear other people talk about 'making love' on dates. I don't think I should, but . . . ."

These are some of the topics you will examine during this unit.

Session 19

The Other Sex (Dating, Part 1)

"Wow! There are some good looking guys around here that I would like to know better. But I'm shy, bashful, blush easily, and I just don't seem to be able to say the right thing. Maybe someday they will notice me and say something to me. Then all I'll have to do is answer. Sure would be a lot easier that way!"

Do you feel a little like this around the opposite sex? If you do, you're probably like most kids your age. They feel uneasy around people of the other sex at first. But a little time and effort can make a big difference.

To begin, think about questions like: How do I get started? How do I break the ice? And furthermore, should I? Isn't it all right just to run around with the gang?

This lesson will focus on casual dating. Later lessons will introduce other dating situations.

WHAT DOES THE BIBLE SAY?

When God created the first people, He told them, "**Be fruitful and increase in number**" **(Genesis 1:28).** God intends for this to happen within the marriage union **(2:24).** Thus, Scripture links marriage and having babies. Somehow young men and young women meet, get acquainted, and eventually get married.

Some marriages in Bible times were arranged by the parents, and we have no descriptions of dating as we practice it today. God does, however, provide some examples of friendships of young men and young women before marriage.

1. Read **Genesis 29:1-30.** How long did Jacob "date" Rachel before they were married?

___

2. What evidences do you find that Jacob and Rachel loved and respected each other?

___

3. You read **The Book of Ruth** in connection with the friendship of Ruth and Naomi (Session 13). Reread **2:1—4:12** and describe the courtship of Ruth and Boaz.

___

___

___

___

___

4. When Mary became pregnant with Jesus, her "boyfriend" Joseph thought she had been unfaithful **(Matthew 1:18-19).** Even in this situation, how did Joseph plan to show respect to Mary?

___

FRIENDSHIPS TODAY

1. Think of a person of the opposite sex that you would like to date. Listed below are some ideas that may or may not help you get a date with that person. Underline those that you think may work for you.

a. Display a friendly smile.
b. Wink at the person.
c. Try to sit at the same lunch table.
d. Follow the person around the hallways.
e. Send an anonymous note containing "sweet nothings."
f. Say "Hi" as often as possible.
g. Stare constantly at the other person whenever possible.
h. "Show off" in front of the other person.
i. Wear bizarre clothes to attract attention.
j. Ask the other person a low-key question, like "What courses are you taking this semester?"
k. Be friendly and natural as much as possible.
l. Ask another person to introduce you to the person.
m. Send "interested" glances to the person.
n. Ask the person to a party.
o. Call the person on the phone and talk to him or her.

2. Let's assume that you have broken the ice, and are on friendly terms with the other person, what topic would make good conversation? List below some topics that you think would work.

a. ____________________

b. ____________________

c. ____________________

d. ____________________

e. ____________________

f. ____________________

3. Suppose that, in the course of talking with the other person, you find yourself at ease in making conversation. Now you would like to go on a date with this person. What would be some good ways of asking, or hinting, for a date? List some ideas you think might work.

a. ____________________

b. ____________________

c. ____________________

d. ____________________

e. ____________________

f. ____________________

4. Should your very "first date" be a single or double date? Why?

____

____

____

5. List some places where you could go on a first date.

a. ____________________

b. ____________________

c. ____________________

6. How "intimate" do you think you should become on the first date? Justify your answer.

____

____

7. How "intimate" should you get on later dates? Read **1 Corinthians 6:18-20.** Then discuss the following questions:

a. How do we sin against our own body?
b. How is our body the temple for the Holy Spirit?
c. How did God buy us for a price?
d. What does all this mean as far as dating is concerned?

Many young people feel a bit uneasy when they are around people of the opposite sex. Going out on dates will help alleviate this uneasy feeling. It will help us get to know persons of the opposite sex. Then we will have a better chance of finding the "right" mate for life, the one who really matches up with our values and personality.

Remember, God has not only established certain ground-rules for dating. He also gives us His Holy Spirit to keep us on the right track. What a wonderful God!

Do you not know that your body is a temple of the Holy Spirit who is in you, whom you have received from God? You are not your own; You were bought at a price. Therefore honor God with your body.
1 Corinthians 6:19-20

Flee the evil desires of youth, and pursue righteousness, faith, love and peace.
2 Timothy 2:22

Session 20

Serious Stuff (Dating, Part 2)

In our last lesson, we discussed some of the aspects of casual dating. Today we will discuss dating that has more serious aspects to it—prolonged dating and going steady.

"Going steady" may be preceded or followed by a lengthy term of "prolonged dating"—a time when you are still going with the person on a regular basis, but are "permitted" to date others.

Let's take a look at serious dating, and identify some of its strengths and weaknesses. Let's also try to identify some of the reasons young people today engage in serious dating.

"CHRIST'S LOVE COMPELS US . . ."

1. You studied **2 Corinthians 5:11-21** in Session 16. Copy the summary statement you wrote at the end of that section. This statement tells how you get the power to forgive those who sin against you.

____

____

2. Apply that power to your relationships on a date. How does the love of Christ affect your attitude and actions toward the person you're dating?

____

____

____

____

3. Read **John 15:1-8.** According to Jesus' words here, what's the key to being able to show love and respect to the person you're dating?

____

____

____

____

"GOING STEADY"

1. List all the reasons you can think of why young people want to date one another.

a. ______________________________

b. ______________________________

c. ______________________________

d. ______________________________

e. ______________________________

f. ______________________________

g. ______________________________

h. ______________________________

i. ______________________________

2. List all the reasons you can think of why young people would want to go steady.

a. ______________________________

b. ______________________________

c. ______________________________

d. ______________________________

e. ______________________________

f. ______________________________

g. ______________________________

h. ______________________________

i. ______________________________

3. Were any reasons given in both activities? If so, what were they? Why did they appear in both lists?

4. What are some of the problems that can occur because of going steady? Ask someone to list these on the board.

5. How can you deal with those problems—what are "some things that work"? Ask someone to list these on the board, too.

6. One of the hazards of "going steady" is the

problem of "breaking up." List some of the major causes of "breaking up."

a. ____________________

b. ____________________

c. ____________________

d. ____________________

e. ____________________

f. ____________________

g. ____________________

h. ____________________

7. List some of the feelings that people experience when they break up.

a. ____________________

b. ____________________

c. ____________________

d. ____________________

e. ____________________

f. ____________________

g. ____________________

h. ____________________

8. What, if anything, can be done about these feelings and the pain they might inflict?

9. Which way would you stand a better chance of finding your mate for life—by "going steady" or "playing the field"? Discuss the advantages and disadvantages of each.

10. Discuss the use of prayer as you try to find the right mate.

Most young people experience lots of joy, but also lots of grief, especially in connection with relationships with the other sex. Learning to relate comfortably with the other sex takes time, and maybe even a little pain. But most people agree that it's worth it. You won't likely find the right mate for life without the "growing up" experiences of the teen years. As you "get serious" about finding your life's mate, pray daily that God would lead you to one who will be a blessing to you.

Love is patient, love is kind. . . . It keeps no record of wrongs. . . . It always protects, always trusts, always hopes, always perseveres.

1 Corinthians 13:4-7

If anyone is in Christ, he is a new creation; the old has gone, the new has come! All this is from God, who reconciled us to Himself through Christ and gave us the ministry of reconciliation.

2 Corinthians 5:17-18

Don't have anything to do with foolish and stupid arguments because you know they produce quarrels.

2 Timothy 2:23

Session 21

Premarital Sex

The material in the following section has been taken from *Lord of Life, Lord of Me* by Bill Ameiss and Jane Graver. (St. Louis: CPH, © 1982. Used by permission.)

LORD OF LIFE, LORD OF ME

Situation 1: *Ruthie and I went steady for about two years. We thought we loved each other and sincerely intended to get married someday. After we broke up I felt pretty guilty about the heavy petting we had done. Even though we never had intercourse, we came close to it many times.*

I've asked God to forgive me, and I know He has. But somehow I don't FEEL forgiven. Why do my guilty feelings keep coming back? Will I always feel guilty about Ruthie, even after I marry someone else?

It is unlikely that the guilt you feel now will be a problem later in your marriage if you realize you have faced your sin and have been forgiven; you are free to go on with the business of living.

However, you will probably always regret what happened between you and Ruthie. The love you two felt for each other was an honest, real emotion, a gift of God. But the way you expressed that emotion was both wrong and unwise.

It is foolish to assume that teenage love will last forever. Most people have so many new experiences during their teens that they almost certainly will change—in an unpredictable direction. The teenage relationship may well last—but it may not.

Because you acted on the assumption that your feelings would not change, you hurt Ruthie and yourself. God's forgiveness does not instantly erase all consequences. Only time—and God—can heal the emotional damage that happens when people invest so much of themselves in a relationship that does not work out. (Page 63)

Situation 2: *How can I get the willpower to say "this far and no further," and stick to it? I feel so guilty sometimes, even though I have never gone all the way.*

You need to talk to God about those guilt feelings. Remember, there is no sin so terrible that you cannot ask for—and receive—His forgiveness. He will never, for any reason, stop loving you.

Whatever you've been doing that you feel guilty about—don't do it! Of course that isn't as easy as it sounds, especially when willpower is something you feel you lack. You probably have the will but not the power.

The good news is, the power doesn't have to come from you. The power comes from the Christ who died for you and rose again. He lives in you. The closer you are to Him, the more power you will have. So read your Bible, pray, commune with Him in His Supper. As you get ready to go out on a date, ask Him to be with you—and trust in *His* power, not your own.

The power He gives you is not a matter of gritting your teeth and being superserious. When things get too intense on a date, often a little humor will relieve the tension. Or you can explain to your date, quite seriously, that you care too much about him (her) to let anything happen you'd both regret. (Pages 63-64)

Too Far, Too Soon

I don't do the good I want to do; instead, I do the evil that I do not want to do . . . To be controlled by human nature results in death; to be controlled by the Spirit results in life and peace.

Romans 7:19; 8:6 TEV

What happens to my good intentions when I'm with her? Why does my desire for her override everything else? Because I am so much in love with her, I forget plans for the future—my parents' love for me—my own deep knowledge of right and wrong.

At least I *think* I'm in love. When we are together, I always want to be close to her. She's the kindest, most fun, prettiest girl I've ever met. Being with her is wonderful. Is that love? Will I still feel the same way five years from now?

I wonder how she feels about our growing closer together. What does she really want? I know we shouldn't go on like this, but what will she think if I back off now? Maybe we should talk about what our limits ought to be—but I wouldn't know how to begin.

God, thank You for my sexuality, for the body you have given me. But I need more! For one thing, I need your forgiveness for so often misusing Your gifts. I need Your support, Your wisdom as I turn around and begin again. Give me the right words to talk to her about how we feel about each other.

Lord Jesus, I really do want Your Spirit to control my life. Help me remember that tonight! (Pages 107-108)

Not Far Enough?

This means that He had to become like His brothers in every way. . . . And now He can help those who are tempted, because He Himself was tempted and suffered.

Hebrews 2:17-18 TEV

Is there something wrong with me? Am I incomplete, Lord? Unmasculine? What do other people say about me behind my back? Do they call me queer? Or cold? Or stupid?

Does everyone else really do it? Is it as great as they claim? Am I missing something wonderful by waiting? Lord, when they joke about the girls they've been with, I don't know what to say. Usually I pretend not to understand their questions—or I kid around with them, say something they can take any way they like. Either way, I feel like a fool.

I like girls, Lord. I'm pretty sure that my sex drive is as strong as anybody's. And even though I'm careful not to let things go too far, I *want* to be free and warm and loving. And sometimes I feel very unwilling to wait any longer. I want it *now*.

What kinds of feelings did You experience, Jesus, as You were growing up? I have trouble picturing You struggling with problems and temptations like mine—yet I know You were like me in this way and all others.

Help me, Lord, to remember You understand how I feel, so I can talk and questions and confess freely to You—and get Your power to act in Your way. (Pages 110-111)

LET'S TALK ABOUT PREMARITAL SEX

1. "Ruthie's exboyfriend," "Too Far, Too Soon," and "Not Far Enough?" were boys. What if they had been girls. What parts of their problems would still have been the same? What parts might have been different? What differences, if any, would you suggest in the way they should handle their problems?

2. The person in situation 2 was a girl. What differences, if any, would there be in this problem if this person was a boy? What differences, if any, would you suggest for a boy who is trying to cope with this problem?

3. Summarize your opinions. What role does each dating partner have in seeing to it that things don't "go too far"?

Both people:

Boys:

Girls:

4. Ruthie and her boyfriend engaged in heavy petting. What dating suggestions would you give them to keep them from doing this?

5. Review the advice given to the girl in situation 2. Which suggestions seem like they would be most helpful to you? Why?

6. On another sheet of paper write a short letter to "Too Far, Too Soon." Help him handle his problem.

7. In addition to the temptation to "go too far" with his girl friend, "Not Far Enough" has trouble handling his relationships with other guys. What advice can you give him to help him in this area?

8. If you "go too far," and then ask for and receive total forgiveness from God, certain "human" problems still could arise. Name as many as you can.

It's often a real struggle to keep oursleves chaste and pure during our youth. Satan, or own sinful flesh, and the world constantly invite us to "enjoy" immoral living. But God has promised to help us, and He will! Rely upon Him, and not upon your own abilities to resist temptation.

Call upon Me in the day of trouble. I will deliver you, and you will honor Me.

Psalm 50:15

What I do is not the good I want to do; no, the evil I do not want to do—this I keep on doing. . . . The mind of sinful man is death, but the mind controlled by the Spirit is life and peace.

Romans 7:19; 8:6

Session 22

"Love and Respect" or "Just Plain Sex"?

Did you talk to some classmates, your parents, or some other friends about Session 21? If so, did you think of some questions you wish you would have asked? Or did you think of some new ideas for some of the questions in that session? Talk about your questions and ideas now.

LOVE AND RESPECT

1. How do you think people feel about each other after heavy petting or "going all the way"? Do you think they still trust each other as much as they did before?

Why is "trust" such an important ingredient in a meaningful, growing relationship? What are some other words that have almost the same meaning as "trust"? Talk about these questions.

2. "Love" is a basket word in the English language. Its meanings include: admiration, trust, respect, strong affection, physical attraction, and physical involvement (sexual intercourse).

The Greeks had three different words for "love." See if you can find out what each word means.

Agape ____________________

____

Philia ____________________

____

Eros ____________________

____

3. Listed below are seven statements and seven Bible verses. Each statement is related to a passage. First, match the statements and the passages.

The seven statements have a logical progression; one leads to another, which leads to another, etc. In the column under "Order" number the statements in a logical progression.

Bible verses: **John 15:13; John 3:17; Romans 13:10; 1 John 4:20; John 3:16; Ephesians 5:33; 1 John 4:19.**

Statements	*Bible Verse*	*Order*
a. People show their love for other people by respecting them.	________	_____
b. People can love God only because God first loved them.	________	_____
c. God loves all people, whether they love Him or not.	________	_____
d. People show respect for other people by respecting their feelings.	________	_____
e. God sent Jesus into the world to save all people.	________	_____
f. When we respect other people, we show respect for ourselves also.	________	_____
g. People show their love for God by loving other people.		

4. On the basis of the previous activity, discuss the following questions.

a. How much love and respect is being shown when a boy asks a girl (or a girl asks a boy) to go all the way?
b. Does God really love all people, no matter what kind of life they lead?
c. What opinion do we have of ourselves when we invite others to join us in sinful acts?
d. If God is such a loving and forgiving God, why should we bother trying to show love to others?
e. What is the relationship between love and respect?
f. Some people believe that boys should have the opportunity to "sow their wild oats," but girls should remain virgins. How true is this?
g. Compare **Matthew 5:48** with **2 Corinthians 5:14-15.** Which of these passages will help you more when you are tempted? Why?
h. Explain the title of this lesson.

5. List some of the things God has done for us so we might go to heaven someday:

a. ____________________ d. ____________________
b. ____________________ e. ____________________
c. ____________________ f. ____________________

6. Suppose you were asked to list some of the things we must do in order to earn God's love and forgiveness. What would you list?

____

You should have left the line blank. God's love and forgiveness are free. We cannot earn them.

7. List some of the things we want to do to show how much we appreciate God's love for us:

a. ____________________ d. ____________________
b. ____________________ e. ____________________
c. ____________________ f. ____________________

Keeping ourselves sexually pure and decent becomes much easier when we rely upon the power of God, who has already defeated Satan through the death and resurrection of Jesus Christ. God enables us to live God-pleasing lives, and the same God forgives us when we sin. Let the love of God fill you; then respond to that love by loving and respecting others, and not using them for your own selfish pleasure.

Christ's love compels us . . . . He died for all, that those who live should no longer live for themselves but for Him who died for them and was raised again.
2 Corinthians 5:14-15

Love does no harm to its neighbor. Therefore love is the fulfillment of the law.
Romans 13:10

Session 23

Lord of Life, Lord of Me

In Session 21 you read some quotes from the book, *Lord of Life, Lord of Me* by Bill Ameiss and Jane Graver. The title of that book reminds us that the Bible gives us the basis and the standards for our life with God, our relationship with others, and our attitudes about our own sexuality. During our high school years and all through life we can be encouraged by the fact that God really is "Lord of Life and Lord of Me."

AGREE OR DISAGREE

Following are some statements about topics in *Lord of Life, Lord of Me.* After each statement tell whether you agree or disagree. Then support your answer from the Bible, from what you have read somewhere else, from what others have told you, and/or from what you have observed around you in the world. (As you work, remember that if another source disagrees with the Bible, that other source is wrong.)

1. Too often the media today present a view of sexuality that belittles people.

2. The male and female sexual systems show the wonder of God's creation.

3. Our sex organs are ours to use in any way we please.

4. There's no relationship between my sexuality and my health.

5. Because Jesus loves me, I can love others.

6. Playing the field is always better than going steady.

7. Dating is a good way to find out if I really love another individual.

8. Sexual intercourse outside of marriage is wrong.

9. Love provides the key to happy sexual experiences of married people.

10. God approves of homosexuality.

11. Abortion is murder, and therefore it is wrong.

12. If a teenage girl gets pregnant, the boy has no responsibility toward that child.

From Him and through Him and to Him are all things.

Romans 11:36

He who did not spare His own Son, but gave Him up for us all—how will He not also, along with Him, graciously give us all things?

Romans 8:32

Do you not know that your body is a temple of the Holy Spirit, who is in you, whom you have received from God? You are not your own; you were bought at a price. Therefore honor God with your body.

1 Corinthians 6:19-20

The fruit of the Spirit is love, joy, peace, patience, kindness, goodness, faithfulness, gentleness and self-control.

Galatians 5:22-23

Session 24

A Timeless Story

Stories. Some are true. Some are fiction. Some fiction stories are based on true stories. Some are old. Some are new. Some are historical. Some are contemporary. And some are timeless.

The best timeless story is true. It tells of God's love for us. God created the first people in His image. When they sinned, He promised them a Savior. He kept that promise, and through that act He saves us from sin, death, and the devil. This is a happy, wonderful, timeless story.

Today we will look at another timeless story. This one is true, too. But it's not happy. It shows the depravity of the human heart. It undoubtedly begins before the great flood of Noah's day. It continued throughout Bible times. And it continues today. Two characters appear in the story: a woman practicing the "oldest profession in the world" and a man—no, a fool. (A fool, you see, is a person who knows what is right, and does the wrong thing anyhow!)

PROSTITUTION

Read **Proverbs 7:1-27.**

1. Notice the strategy of the adulteress (prostitute).

a. What kind of person was she going to seduce **(verse 7)**?

____

____

b. How could someone identify her as a prostitute **(verses 10-12)**?

____

c. How did the prostitute seduce the young man **(verses 13-21)**?

____

____

2. The young man may have felt that this was one of the happiest days of his life. How does God describe him, though **(verses 22-23)**?

____

____

3. What does **verse 25** tell about God's attitude toward prostitution?

____

4. What are some of the consequences of prostitution **(verses 26-27)**?

____

5. Think of reasons why prostitutes seek men and why men seek prostitutes. How much love and respect do you find in these reasons?

____

____

6. God also warns against adultery in **Proverbs 5.** Describe the contrast he uses in **verses 3 and 4.**

____

____

7. What weapons does God mention in **7:1-4** to help us stay away from the adulteress?

____

____

8. Persons who have sexual relations with people other than their spouse run the risk of venereal diseases. Tell what you know about:

Gonorrhea ______________________________

____

____

____

Syphilis ________________________________

____

____

____

Genital herpes ___________________________

____

____

____

9. Describe the tests and cures for the above venereal diseases.

10. How can you tell if a person has VD?

11. Read **2 Timothy 3:16-17.** Why do you think God included **Proverbs 7** in the Bible? (See also **Deuteronomy 5:29.**)

A BETTER STORY

1. Do you recall the story of Ruth and Boaz **(Ruth 2:1—4:17)**? Compare the love and respect you found there with the love and respect you found in **Proverbs 7.**

2. We find an example of love and respect of a husband (Elkanah) and wife (Hannah) in **1 Samuel 1:1-23.** What did Elkanah do for Hannah in:

verse 5?

verse 8?

verse 23?

3. "Be like Ruth." "Be like Boaz." "Be like Elkanah." That's good advice. Unfortunately, when we try to do this on our own, what happens **(Galatians 5:17; 19-21)**?

4. How are we able to "be like" Ruth, Boaz, and Elkanah **(Galatians 5:16, 18, and 22-26)**?

All Scripture is God-breathed and is useful for teaching, rebuking, correcting and training in righteousness, so that the man of God may be thoroughly equipped for every good work.

2 Timothy 3:16-17

Live by the Spirit, and you will not gratify the desires of the sinful nature. . . . If you are led by the Spirit, you are not under law.

Galatians 5:16, 18

"Oh, that their hearts would be inclined to fear Me and keep all My commands, so that it might go well with them and their children forever!"

Deuteronomy 5:29

Session 25

Concluding Activities for Unit 4

"I LIKE YOU"

Divide the class into groups of about six students each. Each groups should have an equal (or almost equal) number of boys and girls. All the people in each group should know one another pretty well.

The goal of this activity is for each boy to hear what the girls like about him, and for each girl to hear what the boys like about her.

Pick one student to begin. Each person of the opposite sex should tell one or two things he or she likes about that student. (Other students of the same sex do not participate at this time.) Continue until each group member has heard comments from everyone of the opposite sex.

WORSHIP

Celebrate the gift of sexuality that God has given you with a time of worship.

Use small groups (possibly the same groups you had for the previous activity) to develop plans for the worship. Perhaps each group could also lead the portion of worship they planned.

Before you plan in small groups, decide what elements you want to include in your worship. Then assign one or more of these elements to each group.

Following are some elements to consider for your worship. You and/or your teacher may have additional ideas.

1. One or more Bible readings.
2. One or more songs or hymns (possibly including action songs)
3. A responsive prayer.
4. Responsive words of praise.
5. A skit.
6. A section of Scripture acted out.
7. A meditation.
8. A prayer by one person.

Unit 5

Stewardship of My Life

As God's child you are saved. God promises you happiness in this life and in heaven. He also gives you a responsibility to share the Good News—and to take care of your body. In this unit you will learn some ways to take good care of your body.

Most young people today think they know all they need to know about alcohol, tobacco, and drugs. Just for fun, complete this test to see how much you know.

PRETEST

If the answers are true, circle T. If they are false, circle F.

T F 1. If you drink beer, and never any other kind of alcohol, you will never become an alcoholic.

T F 2. Wine that is brewed incorrectly becomes vinegar.

T F 3. The Bible teaches that people should never use alcohol (except in the Lord's Supper).

T F 4. A small glass of whiskey will warm your body on a cold night.

T F 5. The use of tobacco is a harmless pastime.

T F 6. Chewing tobacco cleans your teeth.

T F 7. The use of alcohol destroys the liver.

T F 8. Alcohol is just as addictive as heroin.

T F 9. Your dentist administers cocaine when he or she pulls a tooth.

T F 10. "Snorting" cocain is definitely non-addictive.

T F 11. Marijuana is not grown in the U.S.; it must be imported.

T F 12. Marijuana will give you a "high," but leaves no undesirable after-effects.

T F 13. One has to use tobacco a long time before it becomes habit-forming.

T F 14. "Downers" are bad, but "uppers" are OK if handled properly.

T F 15. Morphine and heroin are the same drug.

T F 16. Using alcohol must be all right because lots of adults use it on occasion.

T F 17. Breathing smoke from some other person is just as harmful as smoking yourself.

T F 18. If smoking is as harmful as they say it is, adults around me wouldn't smoke.

T F 19. A party isn't any fun unless some "booze" or "pot" is available.

T F 20. The best solution to alcoholism and drug abuse is stricter laws and stricter law enforcement.

Session 26

Alcohol, Tobacco, The Bible, and You

Drugs as we know them today did not exist during Bible times. Neither did tobacco. We find references to alcohol, though (specifically, wine), throughout Scripture, beginning with Noah after the Flood.

WINE IN THE BIBLE

1. "Are Christians permitted to drink wine?" Leaders of various Christian church denominations do not agree on the answer to this question. To help you understand why this confusion exists, read the following Bible verses. Write *yes* or *no* after each verse to tell whether or not the passage suggests that it's OK to drink wine.

Proverbs 20:1 ______________________

Luke 21:34-35 ______________________

Matthew 11:16-19 ______________________

Romans 13:11-14 ______________________

Genesis 1:28-31 ______________________

Galatians 5:19-21 ______________________

John 2:1-11 ______________________

Proverbs 23:31-35 ______________________

Isaiah 5:11-12, 23 ______________________

Isaiah 23:7-8 ______________________

Romans 14:14 ______________________

Psalm 104:14-15 ______________________

1 Timothy 3:1-3, 8 ______________________

2. Now what do you do? Count how many times you wrote *yes* and *no* in the above activity? No. First of all, if you felt that procedure was best, you would need to examine every passage in the whole Bible, not just those listed above. But that's not the way we interpret Scripture.

Obviously, drinking wine often leads to abuses. As we think of those possible abuses, we need to think about our whole relationship with God. Some of the words we used in the last unit in connection with sexual abuse also apply here.

Read **1 Corinthians 6:19-20.** How do those words affect your attitude toward the use of alcohol?

____

____

3. The words of **1 Corinthians 10:31** apply to anything you do. What do they suggest about the use of alcohol?

____

____

4. What guidelines for the use of alcohol do you find in **Romans 14:13-21**?

____

____

____

____

____

5. St. Paul talks about life through the Spirit in **Romans 8:1-17.** What guidelines and encouragement for alcohol use do you find here?

____

____

____

____

THE USE OF ALCOHOL AND TOBACCO

1. Define "alcohol":

____

____

____

2. Identify the three processes by which alcohol is manufactured:

a. ____________

b. ____________

c. ____________

3. What does alcohol do to the body when:
a. used in careful moderation?

____

____

b. used to excess?

____

____

4. If alcohol used in moderation is all right, when does it become excessive?

____

5. How much is too much?

____

6. Are alcoholics born that way, or can a moderate drinker become an alcoholic?

____

____

7. What "benefits," if any, are derived from drinking?

____

8. What "dangers" are connected with drinking?

____

____

9. What is tobacco?

____

10. Name the three ways tobacco is used.

1. ____________

2. ____________

3. ____________

11. Over a period of years, what effects does tobacco, used in any way, have on the human body?

____

____

12. How addictive is tobacco?

____

13. Since tobacco was not used in Bible times, there is no specific reference to it found in Scripture. But how do you think **1 Corinthians 6:19** and the passages you studied early in this session apply with regard to the use of tobacco? ____________

____

Almost all scientific studies agree that tobacco is definitely addictive and harmful. Alcohol, when used in careful moderation, apparently does not harm the body. But alcohol has a way of growing in usage as time passes, and excessive use of alcohol is definitely harmful to the human body.

As Christians, we have a God-given responsibility to take care of our bodies to the best of our ability. Let's show God that we appreciate His gift of life to us by taking care of our bodies so that we can serve Him with joy and gladness.

You were bought at a price. Therefore honor God with your body.

1 Corinthians 6:20

Whether you eat or drink or whatever you do, do it all for the glory of God.

1 Corinthians 10:31

Session 27

Alcohol, Tobacco, You, and Others

Most people can recall quite clearly "the *first* time" they did anything, or received anything. Do you remember your *first* bicycle? Or roller skates? Or full length dress? Or your first kiss? Or your first cigarette? Or your first beer?

If you haven't tried the last two items yet, chances are that someone, somewhere, sometime will invite you to join them in having one. What will be your response? How will you handle it?

WHAT IF . . . ?

Listed below are two "what if" situations. Place yourself in the situation, use your imagination, and write down how you honestly think you would handle it. Then identify the "feelings" you had during the situation.

1. What if, on the way home from school, your friend, whom you have known for a long time, suddenly pulls out a pack of cigarettes, lights up, and offers you one?

I would ____________________

____

When I was offered the cigarette, I experienced the following feelings: ____________________

____

____

2. What if you were visiting your friend's home on a Saturday afternoon, and your friend's parents suddenly announced that they were going out for the evening and wouldn't be back until around midnight . . . and after they left, your friend went to the refrigerator and got out a few cold beers, and offered you one? You knew you were "under age."

I would ____________________

____

When I was offered the beer, I experienced the following feelings: ____________________

____

____

MY CHRISTIAN CONSCIENCE

1. Look back at your statements on how you felt in the two hypothetical situations. Your Christian upbringing led you to have the feelings you were experiencing. In a very real way, your Christian conscience was at work. Right now, here in class, work together with your instructor, and come up with a good definition of the word, "conscience." CONSCIENCE is:

____

____

____

____

2. Now place the word "Christian" in front of "conscience" and redefine; a "CHRISTIAN CONSCIENCE" is: ___

___

___

3. According to **1 Peter 3:21,** what's the connection between baptism and a good conscience?

___

4. Read **Hebrews 9:14.** What does the blood of Christ do for our consciences?

___

5. What is the purpose of your conscience?

___

6. God gave everyone a natural knowledge of His Law. Therefore by nature everyone has a guilty conscience when he or she does something wrong **(Romans 2:15).** But things change. What happens to the conscience of people who live sinful lives **(Titus 1:15)**?

___

___

7. How can you decide whether you should listen to your conscience when it speaks to you?

___

8. How does a person's conscience become stronger? (Review what you know about the means of grace. Also see **Hebrews 9:14** and **1 Peter 3:21** again.)

___

___

9. How did God show His love for us when He gave us a conscience?

___

___

10. How will our Christian conscience help us when we are confronted with peer pressure?

___

___

___

11. According to your Christian conscience at this moment, what is your position on the use of alcohol?

___

___

___

___

12. On the use of tobacco? ___

___

___

___

13. What should you do if your home environment is telling you one thing, and your Christian conscience is telling you something else?

___

___

___

In our "rubbing elbows" with other people, we will often be confronted with views and ideas that differ from ours. God has placed inside every one of us a still small voice called conscience. It helps us make God-pleasing decisions to His honor and glory because it is His Word that guides and directs our conscience. Be sure to listen to your conscience when it speaks to you. It really is God speaking to you.

"Speak, Lord, for your servant is listening."

1 Samuel 3:9

How much more, then, will the blood of Christ, who through the eternal Spirit offered Himself unblemished to God, cleanse our consciences from acts that lead to death, so that we may serve the living God!

Hebrews 9:14

This water symbolizes baptism that now saves you also—not the removal of dirt from the body but the pledge of a good conscience toward God. It saves you by the resurrection of Jesus Christ.

1 Peter 3:21

Session 28

Pills, Pot—Pleasure, Poison

We live in a world of pills. Our medicine chests are full of them. The TV, radio, and newspaper ads tell us that pills can cure anything and everything. The American public consumes tons of aspirin every year. Without even noticing it, we begin to believe that problems need pills, and pills cure problems—all kinds of problems. Pills cure skin problems, weight problems, sleep problems, boyfriend problems, girlfriend problems. You name it; there's a pill for it.

But there's a big difference between pills prescribed by a physician and "street stuff." Today our lesson focuses on "street stuff" and what it does to your body.

MY BODY/GOD'S BODY

1. Think back to the things you talked about in Unit 1. Who made you? Who redeemed you? Who takes care of you? Who loves you? Who knew all about you while you were still in your mother's womb?

____

2. In what sense can you say that your body belongs to you?

____

3. In what sense can you say that it belongs to God?

____

4. Several times in this course you have studied **1 Corinthians 6:19-20.** Summarize what these verses say about "my body/God's body."

____

____

____

GOD, DRUGS, AND ME

1. While Jesus was on the cross, he refused to drink a mixture of wine and gall **(Matthew 27:34).** Wine, of course, is alcohol, and gall was apparently some kind of drug. Why do you think Jesus refused to drink this mixture?

____

2. Let's assume that you want to take good care of your body. Which of the following would help you most? Rank the choices from 1 to 8, with 1 being the most helpful and 8 the least helpful.

____ Join a health club.
____ Eat "health" foods.
____ Eat a balanced diet.
____ Get plenty of exercise.
____ Take vitamins.
____ Take pills to control my weight.
____ Eat junk food.
____ Get plenty of rest.

3. The world contains many "natural" drugs and many "synthetic" drugs. Natural drugs come from plants or trees. They are grown, harvested, and processed. Synthetic drugs are manufactured from chemicals in a laboratory. Why do we have drugs in our world?

____

____

____

4. Some drugs are stimulants (uppers) and some are sedatives (downers). Identify the following drugs as uppers (U) or downers (D).

____ Cocaine
____ Heroin
____ Barbiturate
____ Valium
____ Morphine
____ Amphetamine
____ Quaaludes
____ Caffeine
____ Methamphetamine
____ Benzedrine

5. Which are more addictive—uppers or downers? Defend your answer.

____

____

____

6. What is the difference between physical addiction and psychological addiction?

____

____

____

7. Which addiction is easier to recover from?

____

8. Why do drug users increase their intake of drugs over a period of time?

____

9. What is "cold turkey"?

____

____

10. What do you know about marijuana (pot)? Is it as bad as some say it is, or does it just provide "kicks"?

____

____

____

11. Some adults say that drugs don't *really* give pleasure. Rather, they are just a poison—a slow, painful, miserable trip that leads to an early grave. Is this statement true, partly true, or false? Defend your answer.

____

____

____

____

____

12. How can you use drugs to the glory of God **(1 Corinthians 10:31)**?

____

____

____

13. Suppose one of your friends has gotten involved with drugs and comes to you for help. He or she feels very guilty for using drugs and for things that happened while on drugs or wanting to get drugs. How will you help your friend "kick the habit"?

____

____

____

____

____

14. How will you help this friend feel good about himself or herself again?

____

____

____

____

____

Do you not know that your body is a temple of the Holy Spirit, who is in you, whom you have received from God? You are not your own; you were bought with a price. Therefore honor God with your body.
1 Corinthians 6:19-20

Whether you eat or drink or whatever you do, do it all for the glory of God.
1 Corinthians 10:31

Session 29

Pills, Pushers, Pals, and Pathos

Here is a conversation that could have taken place in a high school corridor some years ago.

"Hey, Sally, what's that? I didn't know you were sick. Are you taking something for a cold?"

"No, it's not for a cold. And don't talk so loud! These make me feel great. Want one?"

"What is it?"

"It's just a pill—sort of peps me up. Here, take one."

"No, I don't think so. I feel OK the way I am."

"Well, all right. But if you ever want to try some, just let me know."

"Sally, do you know what you're doing? Where did you get this stuff? What's going on? I've never seen you do stuff like this before."

"Oh, Beth! Don't be so uptight. They're just some uppers. You don't get hooked on uppers. They make me feel great. And besides, I got them cheap. I met this girl at a party the other night, and she . . ."

"Can you imagine what you might be doing to your body, getting hooked, or even getting poisoned? I've heard that sometimes . . . ."

"Cool it, Beth. Don't preach to me. If you don't want any, that's OK with me. You always have been a little square. You never want to try anything new. So here we go again. Same old Beth!"

DRUGS AND ME

1. Suppose the above conversation happened in your school. What things would be different?

____

____

____

2. What things would stay the same?

____

____

____

3. How do drugs spread through a school? Maybe Janice introduces Mary to them, who offers some to Tammy, who gets Kathy to try some, and she offers some to Sally, who offers some to Beth. And so it goes. On and on.

People don't try drugs so they can get "hooked." So why do they try drugs? What are some reasons?

____

____

4. The following people had something in common: Jimi Hendrix, Janis Joplin, Marilyn Monroe, Elvis Presley, William Holden, Jim Morrison, John Belushi, Judy Garland, Bruce Lee, David Kennedy, Lenny Bruce. What was it?

They all ______________________________

____

5. Add some more names to the list. __________

____

____

6. Fill in the blanks in the following paragraph:

Lots of people offer drugs to others because they want ________. If you become addicted to drugs, your supplier will be happy, because he or she will have a regular source of ________. If there weren't so much ________involved in the sale of drugs, lots of people wouldn't bother. At first a supplier may *give* you drugs, but after while he or she wants ________. A user at first may have enough ________for his or her habit, but as the habit grows, more and more ________will be needed. In order to get enough ________to satisfy the growing habit, the user may decide to steal, or rob, or become a prostitute. If prostitution is resorted to, usually a pimp will get into the scene for a percentage of the ________. The illicit drug market brings in bushels of ________every year, and most of it ends up with illegal organizations (for example, the Mafia). These organizations use the ________to gain control of more and more of the world's goods. The ________comes from ________who can't or won't say ________to a simple offer.

The Bible says that the love of ________is the root of all kinds of evil **(1 Timothy 6:10).** Jesus says that if you seek His kingdom and rightousness first, ______ ________ ________ will be given to you as well **(Matthew 6:33).** When Solomon asked for wisdom, God gave him ________also **(1 Kings 3:13).** So we don't need to worry about ________. We don't need to help groups like the Mafia. We can say ________when offered some "good stuff."

7. Here are more "what do you do if's":

a. What if a close friend offers you some "good stuff"? What would you do? (Check one or write your own.)

____Ask where it came from.
____Ask what it is.
____Say, "No thanks."
____Smash your friend in the mouth.
____ ________________________________

What was the reason for your choice?

____

b. What if you know some of your classmates are using drugs? What would you do? (Check one or write your own.)

____Tell the principal.
____Tell some of your friends.
____Look the other way and do nothing.
____Join them and get in on the action.
____ ________________________________

What was the reason for your choice?

____

c. What if you notice that the only friends you have are those who use drugs? What would you do? (Check one or write your own.)

____Transfer to another school.
____Try to get some more students in your crowd.
____Seek professional help.
____Tell your parents.
____ ________________________________

What was the reason for your choice?

____

8. You probably made some idealistic choices in the previous question. Can you live up to those choices?

Look at the Bible passages you studied in Sessions 26—28. Then tell why you can hope to live up to the choices you made.

____

____

____

____

____

9. Although you have worked through several "situations" in this lesson, if and when a "real life" situation comes your way, you still may not know what to do. Here are a few basic suggestions that may help you:

—Stay cool and say "no."

—Seek help by talking about the situation with an adult or friend you trust and respect.

—Seek help and guidance from your church (pastor, youth worker, teacher).

—Pray for help and believe that God will help you, because He will. And when you pray, tell God exactly how you feel. He can handle *any* feeling you have!

List another suggestion to share with your class.

____

____

____

God is faithful; He will not let you be tempted beyond what you can bear. But when you are tempted, He will also provide a way out so that you can stand up under it.

1 Corinthians 10:13

Seek first His kingdom and His righteousness, and all these things will be given to you as well.

Matthew 6:33

Session 30

Concluding Activities for Unit 5

A USER OF DRUGS?

1. Divide the class into groups of about six students each. Each group should develop a description of a typical person for each of the following:

a. A person who is vulnerable to drug, alcohol, or tobacco abuse. By human standards, this person will become an abuser someday.

b. A person who is not vulnerable to drug, alcohol, or tobacco abuse. By human standards, this person will never abuse drugs, alcohol, or tobacco, and may not even experiment with them.

c. A person who "innocently" experimented with drugs and eventually became an addict of "hard" drugs. The description should tell how this person changed at each step along the way. Also tell why this person made these changes.

2. Someone from each group should read his or her group's descriptions to the class.

3. Others in the class should evaluate each group's descriptions. In what ways are they accurate? How should they be changed? (Note that we can identify some characteristics of typical drug, alcohol, and tobacco abusers, but that not every abuser is "typical." We ALL need to guard against becoming victims of abuse.)

4. Individually write a prayer in which you ask God to keep you from drug, alcohol, and tobacco abuse. Volunteers may pray their prayers aloud.

Unit 6

My Relationships with My Parents

What are some of the best times you remember ever having with your parents? What are some of the best times you have had during the past week? Answer these questions on a separate sheet of paper.

What are some of the worst times you remember ever having with your parents? What are some of the worst times you have had during the past week? Write these answers on a separate sheet of paper, too.

Compare your answers. What do you think made the good times good? the bad times bad? Be ready to talk about this during class.

Session 31

Parents and Children—God's Plan

God placed people in families. When you were very young, you didn't question this arrangement. After all, as a tiny infant you couldn't change your own diapers or prepare your own food. You undoubtedly felt love toward your parents when they helped you learn to walk, to talk, to pray, to ride a bicycle, and to tie your shoes.

But maybe things seem different now. Maybe you sometimes feel that your parents don't understand you—otherwise they would let you live the way you want to, and not they way they want you to. Instead of always feeling love, maybe you actually hate your parents once in a while.

AUTHORITY AND RESPONSIBILITY

1. Do you ever wish you had more authority? Maybe you wish you could tell the coach which plays to run during a football game or that you could give the homework assignments for some of your classes. Pretend for a moment that you have that authority. What responsibilities would you also have?

____

____

2. God gave parents authority over their children. In **Deuteronomy 6:4-9** He lists a responsibility that goes with this authority. What is it?

____

3. Read **1 Samuel 2:22-25; 3:11-14; 4:10-18.** What happened when Eli failed to carry out his responsibilities as a parent?

____

4. Samuel's sons did not walk in their father's ways **(1 Samuel 8:1-3).** What happened as a result **(8:4-5)**?

____

____

5. In **Genesis 37:3-4** God tells about the favoritism Jacob showed to Joseph. What happened as a result **(37:12-36)**?

____

____

6. What does God say about authority and responsibility in the following passages?

Proverbs 22:6 ______________________________

Ephesians 6:4 ______________________________

1 Timothy 3:4 ______________________________

Proverbs 13:24 ______________________________

Proverbs 19:18 ______________________________

Proverbs 23:13 ______________________________

Deuteronomy 31:13 ______________________________

7. Summarize what God says about parental authority and responsibility.

____

____

____

8. Divide your class into pairs. Each pair should roleplay a conversation between a parent and a teenager in which there is a conflict caused by a disagreement over authority and responsibility. One member of each pair should play the role of a parent, and the other should be a teenager. After about three minutes, change roles.

9. As a class talk about the roleplays. How did it feel to play the role of a parent? What new insights, if any, did you get into the way parents feel? How might this activity change the relationship you have with your parents?

"MY FAMILY AND ME"

1. Take the following inventory. Read each statement carefully and thoughtfully. If you feel that the state-

ment generally applies to your relationship with your parents, check the statement; then list an example from "real life" to tell why you think it applies.

____ a. My parents are concerned that I develop a strong personal relationship with Jesus Christ. Example:

____ b. My parents like to pry into my private life; that irritates me. Example:

____ c. My parents show respect for both me and my opinions. Example:

____ d. My parents usually find something wrong with the friends I pick. Example:

____ e. My parents are willing to take time to talk with me about my problems, plans, questions, accomplishments, etc. Example:

____ f. My parents and I enjoy being around one another and doing things together. Example:

____ g. My parents are constantly "nagging" at me. Example:

____ h. My parents usually think that they are never wrong in either their actions or opinions. Example:

____ i. My parents tend to treat me like I am still a small child. Example:

____ j. My parents "come down hard" on me when I do something wrong. Example:

2. This inventory gives you some idea of how you think of the way your parents treat you. What are some other things—things not mentioned in the inventory—that affect your attitude toward your parents?

3. What are some things you like about the relationship you have with your parents?

4. What are some things about your relationship with your parents that you wish were different?

For now, think and pray about the things you wrote. At another time you may want to talk with your parents about them, but wait until later in this unit.

Children, obey your parents in the Lord, for this is right. "Honor your father and mother"—which is the first commandment with a promise—"that it may go well with you and that you may enjoy long life on the earth." Fathers, do not exasperate your children; instead, bring them up in the training and instruction of the Lord.

Ephesians 6:1-4

Train a child in the way he should go, and when he is old he will not turn from it.

Proverbs 22:6

Session 32

"My Family" and "God's Family"

Think about the people you know who are about your age. Which one do you think has the happiest family life? Why do you think this family is happy?

____

____

If possible, talk with this person. Find out his or her views about things that make their family life happy. List ideas for a happy family life that you get from this person.

____

____

"MY FAMILY" AND "GOD'S FAMILY"

1. God sometimes compares His family, the Church, to a human family. Read **Ephesians 3:14—4:32.** What key to happiness do you find in each of the following verses?

3:16 _______________

3:17 _______________

4:2 _______________

4:3 _______________

4:7-13 _______________

4:15 _______________

4:25 _______________

4:26 _______________

4:27 _______________

4:28 _______________

4:29 _______________

4:31 _______________

4:32 _______________

2. Which of those keys to happiness apply to human families?

____

____

____

3. Which of those keys to happiness do you especially wish was present in your family in greater measure than it is?

____

____

4. Undoubtedly you cannot control some of the keys to happiness you listed in #3. Someone else in your family must change in order for those things to happen. But you probably can do some things to change other keys to happiness. List some of the things you can change. Also tell what you can do to cause this change. (Answer this question on another sheet of paper. You need not share your answer.)

5. In the next session we will discuss communication within your family. With good communication you *may* be able to help others in your family (including your parents) change some of the behaviors that bother you. List some ideas you have now about ways you can help others in your family make some of these changes.

____

____

____

TENSION IN FAMILIES

Many things can cause tension in families. Today we'll look at pressures that affect your parents. Then, in session 33, we'll look at some conflicts between parents and teenagers.

1. Both parents in this family have jobs outside the home. Both jobs require lots of time and energy. As a

result, everyone is tired almost every evening. They (and you) manage to do everything that needs to be done around the house, but sometimes tempers are short. Sometimes your family's conversations don't go much beyond, "Whose turn is it to do the dishes?" or "What shall we watch on TV tonight?"

a. Tell how the pressures on the parents affect the teenager(s) in the family.

____

____

b. How can a teenage child help these parents handle the pressures they face?

____

____

2. These parents are planning to get a divorce. They're usually civil to each other when any children are around, but the teenage child often hears them argue late at night. Communication exists between parents and children, but it seems to be forced.

a. How do the pressures of an upcoming divorce affect the teenagers in the family?

____

____

b. How can a teenage child help these parents handle the pressures they face?

____

____

3. The mother in this home is an alcoholic. Again and again she has vowed to quit, but it seems like almost anything leads her to take another drink—and go on another binge. She drinks when she's happy, she drinks when she's angry, she drinks when she's bored. When she's sober, she is very pleasant, but too often she is yelling at her husband and children.

a. How does this alcohol problem affect the teenage children in this family?

____

____

b. How can a teenage child help this mother?

____

____

c. How can a teenage child help the father in this home?

____

____

4. The parents in this home were divorced over five years ago, and the mother is raising the children alone. She has a fair job, but the father seems to always be behind in child support and alimony payments. Therefore the mother takes in typing at night to supplement her income. She tries to provide time for her children, but again and again her time and energy do not permit her to spend much time with them.

a. How do this mother's problems affect her teenage children?

____

____

b. How can a teenage child help this mother handle the pressures she faces?

____

____

5. Pretend the teenager in one of these situations is your best friend. On another sheet of paper write a letter of encouragement to him or her.

Be kind and compassionate to one another, forgiving each other, just as in Christ God forgave you.
Ephesians 4:32

Speaking the truth in love, we will in all things grow up into Him who is the Head, that is, Christ. From Him the whole body, joined and held together by every supporting ligament, grows and builds itself up in love, as each part does its work.
Ephesians 4:15-16

Session 33

Communication in My Family

Is it hard to talk to your parents? Do you wish you could have better conversations with them? If you answered "Yes" to these questions, you're like most young people your age.

If you felt sure of yourself, and you thought your parents would listen to your point of view, what are five things you would like to talk to your parents about tonight?

1. ______________________________

2. ______________________________

3. ______________________________

4. ______________________________

5. ______________________________

CHRISTIAN FAMILY COMMUNICATION

1. When God created the first people, they had perfect communication with each other and with God. But they sinned. At once communication problems developed. Adam blamed God and Eve for his sin **(Genesis 3:12).** Their first child became so angry with his brother that he killed him **(4:1-8).**

But God did not abandon us. He sent His Son to save us **(John 3:16).** Because we have again become His children, He gives us the power to overcome the problems of sin. We can again communicate with one another in love. How do we become God's children according to **Galatians 3:26?**

____

2. During the last session you read parts of **Ephesians 3 and 4.** Read **4:1-3** and **15** again. What do these verses say about Christian family communication?

____

____

3. Some Christians use the following 3-step process when they have communication problems with other Christians:

a. Admit my sin.

b. Accept the other person's forgiveness.

c. Offer forgiveness to the other person.

This process often seems threatening, because we don't always like to admit our sin. Instead of saying, "I sinned when I refused to do the dishes," we like to say, "It's normal for teenagers to not want to do the dishes." But if we say, "I sinned, and I'm sorry," it's relatively easy for the other person to say, "I forgive you."

The last step calls for us to offer forgiveness to the other person. What if the other person doesn't ask for our forgiveness? How can you offer forgiveness to your parents, for example, if you think they have sinned, but they don't want to admit it to you? You can offer them forgiveness *in your heart*. Just give it to them. That's the first and most important step for you. It's a step you can't take without God's power in you. But with God's power it's an act very much like the forgiveness God offers you!

Roleplay this 3-step process. Saying the words in a roleplay may make it easier to also say them in real life. Have someone do this once or twice for the whole class. Then talk about it. Finally, form pairs and say the words of confession and absolution to each other.

4. Many people find that their conversations improve when they practice active listening. In active listening a speaker checks out his or her understanding of what the other person said before responding to that statement.

a. Practice active listening. A small group of students might come to the front of the class to discuss some controversial subject. One person says something. Every speaker after that must follow one rule: Before you add something to the conversation, you must repeat the thought of the other speaker until he or she agrees that your paraphrase is accurate.

b. Form small groups and give everyone in the class a chance to practice active listening.

5. We will look at one more communication skill that's helpful for most people: sending "I" messages instead of "you" messages. For example, you would say, "I feel so much better when I wear the same kind of clothes that my friends wear," instead of, "Mother, you're so old-fashioned!"

Practice giving "I" messages. First ask someone to give a "you" message.Then suggest an "I" message that you could use instead.

As you do this, notice how "you" messages often focus on "Who's guilty?" while "I" messages focus on the issues instead. (The same thing happens in active listening.)

In the 3-step confession/forgiveness process described earlier, you focused on confessing instead of accusing. Thus, all three communication skills listed here are designed to move away from accusing, or blaming. (At times, of course, we need to accuse people so they recognize their sin. But accusations are especially counterproductive when part of the problem belongs to US. Good communication often leads others to accuse themselves, a step more useful in relationship than when we accuse them.)

TENSIONS BETWEEN PARENTS AND TEENAGERS

Let's roleplay again. Following are some examples of tensions in families. One person should play the teenager in each example. Another should play a parent. Add details to make the situation realistic. The person playing the teenager with the problem in each situation should roleplay things he or she can do to get rid of some of the tension. Be sure to use the communication skills you discussed in the last section. Also be aware of the tensions the parent might feel.

Then talk about the situation with your classmates. If you come up with different ways for the teenager to handle the situation, roleplay it again. Remember, you want to help him or her cope with the situation. Even if the parents are wrong, you aren't really being very helpful if you help the teenager criticize them.

1. A teenager is upset because his mother always compares him to his "smart" older brother. By really working hard he gets a "B" in algebra. When he proudly shows his grades to his mother, she says, "_______ got an 'A' when he took algebra!"

2. All her life this teenager's father seemed to think he was showing kindness to his daughter because he spent a lot of time with her. But he always took her along to the things HE wanted to do—bowling, football games, etc. Last night she wanted to talk with him about the classes that are being offered next year. He said, "Not now. I don't have time. I have to wash and wax the car."

3. This teenager likes to listen to the latest music on his stereo—turned up loud! As soon as his father comes home from work, he yells, "Turn the music down!" This usually starts a whole night of yelling at each other.

4. This teenager's mother has set an unreasonable curfew—at least that's the way it seems to the teenager. They argue about the curfew almost every weekend, and the arguments really get heated when the teenager comes home late!

Live a life worthy of the calling you have received. Be completely humble and gentle; be patient, bearing with one another in love. Make every effort to keep the unity of the Spirit through the bond of peace.

Ephesians 4:1-3

Speaking the truth in love, we will in all things grow up into Him who is the Head, that is, Christ.

Ephesians 4:15

Session 34

Parents Until . . .

"I've been going with Jill forever. But I'm about ready to quit. She'll talk, talk, talk about other girls. But cars? She won't say a word about cars. I like to talk about cars sometimes. And when she isn't talking about girls, she's sitting in front of the TV. I'm tired of her. I think I'll drop her and find someone else."

"I know what you mean. Reminds me of Maria. Only she talks about food. And eat! You should see her eat! You'd think she'd be as big as a truck, but she still looks like Twiggy! I just traded for a new car. Maybe I should have traded for a new girl instead."

And so it goes. Get a different girl, get a different car, get a different house, get some different clothes . . .

What about parents? How about some "new" parents?

ME AND MY PARENTS

1. At the end of session 31 you listed some "good" and "bad" things about your relationships with your parents. You probably thought more about these relationships in sessions 32 and 33. Have your thoughts changed at all since then? If so, what kinds of changes do you notice?

____

____

____

2. Do you sometimes wish you could trade in your parents for some new ones? When some people feel this way, they run away from home. You might know someone who has run away from home at least once. Maybe you have done this—or at least thought about it. Maybe you know someone right now who is thinking about running away from home. Why do children and teenagers run away from home?

____

____

____

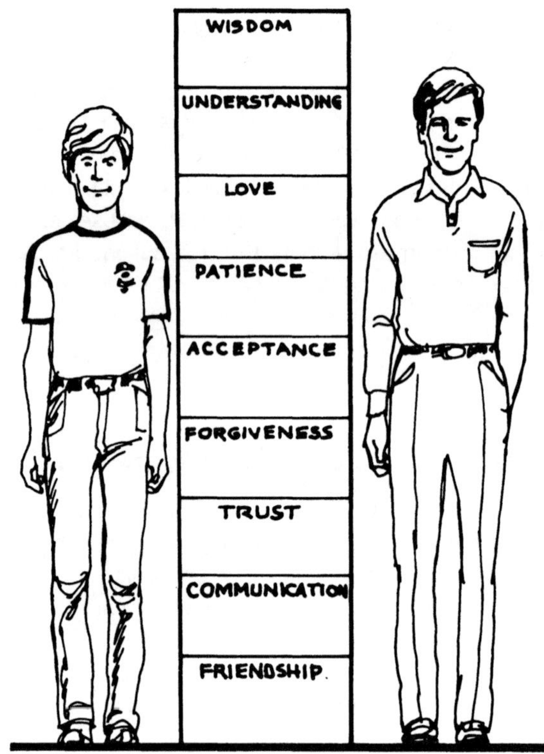

I'M GROWING

3. Use the following statements to help you think through your feelings about parents. Read each statement carefully. If the statement sums up your thoughts or feelings, check it:

____ a. Parents should be seen and not heard.

____ b. Parents make too many mistakes themselves, so they should stop criticizing their children.

____ c. I would really appreciate it if my parents would trust me a little more.

____ d. Most parents expect their children to be perfect.

____ e. Parents have a right to yell at their children because they are parents.

____ f. My parents are simply unreasonable.

____ g. My parents keep treating me like I am still a little child.

____ h. I hardly ever see my parents, and when I do, we hardly ever talk.

____ i. My parents are more interested in their jobs than they are in me.

____ j. I intend to get an apartment for myself as soon as I have some money saved up and get a decent job.

____ k. My parents are far from perfect, but I love them very much.

____ l. My parents always treat my brother(s)/sister(s) nicer than they treat me. I'm sick of it.

____ m. We are not a rich family, but we seem to be pretty happy. At least I'm happy.

____ n. The sooner I get out of my parents' house and on my own, the better I'll feel.

4. Look back over the statements you checked. Do you detect an urge to "split" because of family pressures? Or are you one of the happy teen-agers who enjoys home?

THE LOST SON

Read **Luke 15:11-32** and answer the following questions:

1. Why did the younger son want to get away from home?

2. What kind of a manager was the younger son?

3. How bad did things get?

4. What brought him to his senses?

5. What keeps more people from doing what the younger son did in verses 17-19?

6. What did his father do when he saw him coming home?

7. Why did the father "throw a party"?

8. How did the older son feel?

9. Were his feelings justified?

10. What were the father's reactions toward the older son?

11. The moral of this story is: (pick one)

____Leave home as soon as possible.

____If you want to be great some day, first become a bum.

____Squander your inheritance. There's more where that came from.

____Living a life of sin is OK, because forgiveness has been promised.

____Other: ______________________________

____

PARENTS UNTIL . . .

1. According to **Proverbs 23:22,** when may we forget about listening to our parents?

____

2. Read **Luke 2:51-52.** Why would Jesus, the almighty, perfect Son of God, want to be obedient to Mary and Joseph, who were human beings, sinners, full of error? Why *should* Jesus be obedient? How can a perfect man like Jesus "grow in wisdom" when from all eternity, He already knew everything there is to know? How could Jesus grow in "favor" with God?

3. If you're like most people your age, you sometimes feel like the lost son when he wanted to leave home and get away from his parents. At other times you feel more like he did when he wanted to go back home, or like Jesus when He obeyed Mary and Joseph. Then you want forgiveness for your "bad" thoughts. Why can you be sure God will forgive them?

____

4. How would you go about asking your parents to forgive you? Talk about this question with others in your class. If you have time, roleplay this situation. Be sure to use some of the communication skills you learned in session 33.

5. Think of other things you could do—with God's help and with your parents help and cooperation—to make your home a happier place, a place you won't want to run away from. List some of them on a separate sheet of paper.

6. If you have time, roleplay a conversation with one of your parents. Talk about ways to make your home a happier place. Again, be sure to use some of the communication skills from session 33.

Let us therefore make every effort to do what leads to peace and to mutual edification.

Romans 14:19

Session 35

Concluding Activities for Unit 6

PARENTS

1. Divide the class into pairs. Each person should talk for 30 to 60 seconds about each of the following topics:

a. Things about my parents that bother me
b. What I like about my parents

2. Divide the class into groups of about five each.

a. Each group should pretend they are getting questions ready for a news conference with God. They represent a young person whose parents just got a divorce. They should prepare 10 questions they want to ask God about this situation.
b. Give the questions to another group. This group should answer the questions as they think God might answer them.
c. Share the questions and answers with the whole class.

3. What are some worries that parents have? Each student should select five from the following list. After you finish, tally the answers and talk about the most common worries and possible reasons for these concerns.

Parents worry their teenager will:

a. take drugs
b. get into a fight
c. get expelled from school
d. have to get married
e. fail a class
f. skip school
g. get married too early
h. not get married
i. drink alcohol
j. smoke cigarettes or marijuana
k. have an abortion
l. never get a job
m. join a gang
n. not go to college
o. move out or run away
p. wreck the car

q. not be popular
r. turn into a religious or cultist fanatic
s. other (explain)

Reprinted by permission from *The Youth Group Meeting Guide,* Copyright 1984. Group Publishing, Box 481, Loveland, CO 80539.

MY PARENTS AND ME

1. Divide your class into six groups. Assign one of the following Bible passages to each group. The group should prepare to tell the class how their passage relates to parent/teenager relationships.

a. **Galatians 6:9-10**
b. **Ephesians 4:29**
c. **Ephesians 6:1-4**
d. **Colossians 3:13**
e. **Colossians 3:23-24**
f. **James 1:19**

2. Individually, write a letter to your parents. You might tell them what you like about them and some dreams you have for your family. Also include other things you thought about during this unit—things you really want them to know or things you want to ask them.

3. Practice the communication skills you learned in this unit. Divide into pairs, and take turns playing the roles of a parent and a teenager. Talk about the topics in #3 of the first section of this session or about another issue that causes tension in families.

Unit 7

Go and Tell about Jesus!

Can you imagine Mary of Magdala's overflowing excitement when she ran to Jesus' disciples and joyfully told them, "I have seen the Lord!" after she had talked with Him outside the empty tomb? Do you think Mary told her news loudly? hurriedly? nervously? bubbly? Say those five words of good news to yourself in the voice you think Mary might have used. Describe how you told yourself this good news: ______________________

Jesus gave all of His friends a command: **Go and tell!** Share the good news of His love and forgiveness and gift of eternal life with other people. Think of a time when you had *great* news to tell your friend. How did you tell him or her? How did you feel when you shared your good news?

You'll discover more about the what, when, where, why, and how of telling the Good News of Jesus through this unit.

Session 36

Disciples, Witnesses, and Evangelists

More than 1,000 disciples of Teacher Jeremiah Miller attended a "Teach One-Reach One" retreat last weekend at Camp Highway to Heaven.

"Will Obadiah Jones please take the witness stand? Repeat after me. I, Obadiah Jones, do solemnly swear . . ." Mr. Jones is a witness in the courtroom.

Reverend Ezra Smith just completed a week-long evangelistic rally at the county stadium where he preached to an estimated crowd of 100,000 people. Informed church leaders estimate that over 3,000 people received Jesus Christ as their personal Savior at the end of Rev. Smith's dynamic preaching.

Disciples—witnesses—evangelists. What are they? What do they do? How are they alike and how are they different? Are you one or more of these? Mr. Jones is a witness. So is Evangelist Smith. So is Teacher Miller. Is Mr. Jones an evangelist? And is Evangelist Smith a disciple? Let's find out more about what these words and jobs really mean for us.

DISCIPLES

1. First, write your description of a "disciple." What is one? What does one do?

____

2. Now read these Scripture passages and write the descriptive words for "discipleship" and "disciples."

John 15:16 ______________________________

____

Ephesians 4:15 ______________________________

____

Matthew 28:19-20 ______________________________

____

1 Peter 4:10 ______________________________

____

3. Find some of the characteristics of a disciple from these passages.

1 Timothy 6:11-16 ______________________________

Matthew 16:24 ______________________________

John 8:31 ______________________________

Luke 12:12 ______________________________

John 13:34-35 ______________________________

4. Now that you've read these Scriptural descriptions and characterizations of a disciple, describe any evidence you see of "discipleship" happening among you and your school friends.

5. In what ways do you think you and your friends and your teachers can grow together in "discipleship" so that "discipling" becomes a natural, easy, everyday thing to do?

6. How would you "be a disciple" to a preschool friend? to an elementary school neighbor? to a friend at high school? to your parent(s) or adult guardian(s)? to a grandparent in a nursing home? to your teacher(s)?

WITNESSES

1. Write what you think a witness is and what he or she does. ______________________________

____

2. Read what Jesus says about witnesses in **Acts 1:8.**

According to Jesus, what will happen when God's Holy Spirit comes to you? ______________________________

____

Jesus told His friends that they would be witnesses in Jerusalem, Judea, Samaria, and in all areas of the earth. In what places will you witness? ______________________________

____

3. *Witnessing* is *more* than just a word. And witnessing is more than just a plan on paper or in a book. For you to be an active witness for the Lord means that

you love Him and that you daily include Him in your life's events. You become aware of daily opportunities to share the Good News. You actually feel FREE—free to share how you feel about Jesus dying for your sins and about His making it possible for you to live with Him someday in heaven!

Think about how you feel about God's love and His Son's death for your sake. Can you take the big risk of sharing your feelings? *Will you take the risk and share the Gospel with someone around you?* Make a few notes about how you feel and about how you might take the first big step into your life as a witness for Christ. ______________________________

____

____

EVANGELISTS

1. The word "evangelist" is derived from two Greek words—*eu* which means good and *angelion* which means news. Write a definition of "evangelist" in your own words.

____

____

2. According to **Mark 16:15-16,** what did Jesus tell His eleven friends to do?

____

3. Is every preacher an evangelist? Why or why not?

4. Read **Romans 10:14-15** and tell what distinguishes evangelists from disciples and witnesses.

5. Some witnesses and disciples are, at the same time, evangelists. But not ALL are evangelists. Read **2 Timothy 4:1-5.** What are some of the characteristics of an evangelist according to Paul's message to Timothy?

6. What unusual truth do you read in **Acts 16:6?** Can you think of ways and reasons the Holy Spirit might do this today?

7. Is an evangelist "born," or can he or she be trained as an evangelist? Describe how you could learn to do the work of an evangelist.

LET'S GET STARTED!

All of us are witnesses for Christ Jesus. It's our job to witness for Him as well as we can. It's a good feeling to know that our heavenly Father helps us. He answers our prayers and sends us His power through the Holy Spirit living in us. God lives each of our daily experiences with us and provides His constant guidance. It's assuring to remember that when we do fall short of God's will for us—when we fail to use an opportunity to tell a friend that Jesus loves them and died to save them from their sins—He will forgive us and keep on loving us!

If you discover that you don't have the gifts for being an evangelist, you can pray that God will keep you as His disciple and that He will help you become a better witness for Him. Through the Holy Spirit's work, people know and feel God's love and salvation, whether you're discipling, witnessing, or evangelizing!

God uses you to His honor and glory. Praise and thank Him. And ask Him to help you with whatever work He has for you to do!

A prayer to pray today: *I feel good about my relationship to you, God. I know that you love me and forgive me for Jesus' sake. I'm sure that You'll show me whatever plans You have for me to do Your work. Help me tell others of Your love and forgiveness so they may know You and feel the peace and joy that only Your Spirit gives. Give me whatever I need—the understanding to disciple, the empathy to witness, and the courage to evangelize—for Your glory and honor. Amen.*

You will be His witness to all men of what you have seen and heard.

Acts 22:15

Session 37

Public Ministry or Universal Priesthood?

In today's session, we want to distinguish between two basic groups: the public servant and the private servant. Both are Christians. Both help others. One servant performs acts privately, with no other authority than from God Himself. You and all lay workers are a part of this "universal priesthood of believers." The other servant performs public acts, through the authority granted by the local congregation. Your pastor is part of this public ministry.

Before going any further, read and summarize briefly the following Scripture passages. How do these passages describe the work of public ministers and the people like you who are part of the whole priesthood of believers?

1 Peter 2:9 ______________________________

____

2 Corinthians 5:18-20 ______________________________

____

Acts 6:4 ______________________________

____

Acts 14:23 ______________________________

____

Acts 20:28 ______________________________

____

Many Christians think that only trained, full-time church workers should be involved in proclaiming the Gospel to people, administering the sacraments, visiting sick and shut-in people, and preparing the worship services. But **1 Peter 2:9** reminds us that God has chosen ALL Christians to be His ministers. Each ministers in his or her own unique way. ALL of us are priests before God. We need to take our priestly office seriously and perform the tasks God assigns to us joyfully and willingly. Just as we are never "off duty" as witnesses, neither are we ever relieved of duty as members of Christ's universal priesthood! Through the fullness and guidance of the Holy Spirit, we each can assume responsibility to see that the church and all believers remain faithful to God and do the work He gives us to do.

DARE DEVOTION: When in the World Will We Listen?

Sounds

(This is meant to be a responsive meditation. The leader shall speak the capitalized words; the group shall speak the rest. There are three distinct moods: *Whisper of Meditation, Shout of Faith, and Call to Service.* They should be spoken as indicated.)

Whisper of Meditation (Spoken quietly)

THERE ARE SOUNDS FOR ALL OF US—

the silent sounds unexpressed within me; quiet sounds as I dream of what I'm going to be, sounds which folks and friends won't hear or see.

AND THERE ARE SOUNDS SURROUNDING ME

coming from my own family, arising in my community, enfolding me in reality.

SOME SOUNDS SOOTHE ME

like when I hear my voice spilling troubles to a friend; or hear my parents pledge they love me to the end; or drink in the sounds of music as they blend.

OTHER SOUNDS DISTURB ME

as sirens wail mournful announcements of pain; and newscasts report war's wounded and slain; and worry wraps itself around my brain.

I SOMETIMES WONDER IF I CAN STAND MORE SOUNDS,

for all day long I live with noise that threatens and sometimes destroys my attitudes and thinking, and my poise.

Shout of Faith (Spoken louder with each verse)

YET, AMONG THESE SOUNDS A STRONGER SOUND BREAKS THROUGH—

the powerful sound of God's great might, the sound of God's answer to our plight; the sound of God's call to us in Christ, the Lord: the moving sound of His Holy Word, the sound of God at work in our world.

THE SOUNDS OF WHAT GOD DID FOR US IN CHRIST LIE DEEP IN TIME LONG PAST;

a newborn Baby crying in a stable . . . a young Man fulfilling God's law for folks not able . . . a Man involved with people, teaching, healing, caring; so involved with people in His mission of sharing a holy Father's love for fallen man that nothing could frustrate God's plan.

THE SOUND OF GOD IS A SAVING SOUND.

In agony and prayer at Gethsemane; on a hill, nailed to a tree; through a death that made us free; by rising again for you and for me Christ won life for us in God's family.

BUT IT'S NOT PAST AND GONE, THIS SOUND OF WHAT GOD DID FOR US;

for the sound of His call is broadcast to us today challenging us to leave death and find life in His way. The sound of Christ is not a dead sound echoing in a grave; it is the sound of life His resurrection gave. Christ lives! He comes among us with His peace and promises life which shall never cease. His call to live, though, adds something new: **"As the Father sent Me; so send I you."**

Call to Service (Spoken with conviction)

THIS SOUND IS CALLING US TO MOVE OUT

beyond ourselves—and so become ourselves—being hurled beyond the world we know—that we might live more fully in the world; the new world in the making where boundaries are breaking and separations between nation, language, culture, class, and race and even separations in the church seem really out of place.

THE SOUND OF GOD GOES OUT—GOD'S CALL TO US IN JESUS CHRIST;

to serve and to belong to one another, to worship and to witness to our brother, to share Christ's purpose and receive His power as we live in history's finest (or final) hour.

THE SOUND OF GOD IS A SENDING SOUND

moving us outside of chapel walls, sending us into our school halls; thrusting us back into families, propelling us into communities; Christ calling us in Him, to be: **"I send you, as the Father sent me."**

THE HOLY SPIRIT SENDS US WITH CHRIST'S SOUND TO THE SONS OF MEN;

to families that quarrel and don't know how to forgive, to friends at school who don't know what it means to live, to neighbors who don't know what Christ has to give.

CHRIST'S SOUND SENDS US TO THE WORLD OF MEN

where people feel the reality of pain and sin holds them like a chain in lifeless life's dreary domain.

CHRIST'S SOUND SENDS US TO THE SOUNDS OF MEN—

to children just starting on their ways and old folks near the end of days; to our own group, which studies and plays, and to those trapped in the middle-age maze.

CHRIST'S SOUND SENDS ME PERSONALLY

to share the saving sound of God, to serve them in the way Christ trod; to love them as Christ first loved me that, hearing His grace they may also see the life that lasts eternally.

I pray that you may be active in sharing your faith, so that you will have a full understanding of every good thing we have in Christ.

Philemon 6

So in Christ we who are many form one body, and each member belongs to all the others. We have different gifts, according to the grace given us.

Romans 12:5-6

Session 38

Hey, What About . . .

We Christians face all kinds of social issues and concerns in our attempts to live Jesus' commission for us, "Go and teach them to obey EVERYTHING I have commanded you" **(Matthew 28:20).** At the time of Christ, demon possession was a very real social problem. What issues confront God's family members today? Why is it important for you to find appropriate Scriptural answers to today's current issues if you are to be a good witness of God's family? Can you find active solutions to issues that will please God and let your light shine among the people for Him? Hey, what about . . .

BIRTH CONTROL?

How do you feel about the use in general of any or all methods of birth control? As you mature and perhaps look forward to marrying and enjoying family life, what are some of your personal fears, concerns, attitudes, and beliefs about birth control methods? What are your concerns for the world?

Read what God says to Adam and Eve and then to Noah and his family concerning their family life in **Genesis 1:28 and 9:1.**

How does God instruct these couples? And what promise does He make in **9:3?**

In what way will you, as a Christian, reflect your Christian attitudes and beliefs about birth control to others around you?

ABORTION?

In 1967, the United States Supreme Court declared abortion "a private matter," a decision for the mother-to-be. The Supreme Court legalized abortion in 1973. Is this what God says? Between 1967 and 1985, in the United States alone, more than twenty million unborn children were murdered—intentionally aborted!

Read these Scripture selections for guidance on the issue of abortion: **Psalm 139:13-16; Jeremiah 1:5; Luke 1:15; Luke 1:41-44; Exodus 20:13; Deuteronomy 27:24-25.**

Be prepared to discuss these questions: When does a fetus become alive? When does a fetus become a person? Is an abortion under any circumstance right? What is YOUR stand on the abortion issue?

Did you know that from the beginning, the Lutheran Church—Missouri Synod has taken a firm pro-life, anti-abortion stand? Many public ministers and layworkers join together in upholding Scriptural truths and the right-to-life conviction.

Think of the consequences had these people lived through pro-abortion thoughts, feelings, and actions: Jesus' mother, Mary, and her family; the mothers of J.S. Bach, Martin Luther, and Martin Luther King, Jr.; the mothers of Dr. Louis Pasteur, Dr. Jonas Salk, Beethoven, Loretta Lynn, and YOU!

Write your feelings and convictions about the issue of abortion. Include, also, ways you can and will reach out to others to educate and influence them in this life-or-death matter. What would you say to your sister, mother, or school friend if one of them told you she had made an appointment to have an abortion?

HOMOSEXUALITY?

1. Do you feel people have a choice regarding homosexuality? Why, or why not?

____

2. Read **Romans 1:26-28.** What does God's Word say about homosexuality?

____

3. Now read **Genesis 19:1-29.** What happened in

the cities of Sodom and Gomorrah? How did God act toward these people?

____

____

4. Imagine that a homosexual confronts you at the shopping center. What will you say? What will you do? How will you reach out to that person and witness your Christian beliefs?

How would you reach out to your sister or brother or friend if he or she hesitantly confided to you that he or she felt homosexual feelings but had not yet experienced a homosexual relationship?

If you ever feel tempted to experiment homosexually, with whom could you comfortably talk about your feelings and concerns without feeling guilty and ashamed? Don't hesitate to find a good counselor, through your pastor, principal, or teachers, if you ever feel you need to express yourself privately. You are loved, and many trained people are available to help you through rough times of your life.

PORNOGRAPHY?

1. The production and availability of pornography (sexually suggestive printed and non-printed materials) increases each year. Describe what you think "porno" is: ______________________________

____

____

Can literature be sexually immoral, but not pornographic?

How? ______________________________

____

2. Read **2 Timothy 3:1-4** and tell what words describe the problem of pornography.

____

____

3. It's time for more soul-searching. What can and will YOU do, as a Christian with convictions, about pornography around you? Your friend brings a copy of *Playgirl* to school and keeps it in the locker you share.

You: ______________________________

Your aunt and uncle bring a triple-X rated video cassette to your home to watch with your parents. You:

____

____

The quick-stop store near your school displays pornographic magazines and young children very frequently stop there for ice cream and gum. You:

____

4. You probably know someone who has commited grievous sins in connection with the issues mentioned in this session. Does God still love that person? Does He forgive him or her? If God forgives, should we just keep on sinning—"enjoy life"—because we know that we'll be forgiven anyhow? Thinking of all these questions, what can you say to your friend?

OTHER SOCIAL CONCERNS?

Again, it's impossible to cover in this session everything that socially affects and concerns you as a Christian in this world. But it's important that you are aware of the issues and that you ask yourself, "What do I think of this? And what does God say about that?" It's important that you know the issues, decide on your position as a Christian, and firmly demonstrate to those around you, through your words and actions, your Christian convictions.

List timely issues that concern you and the whole world today:

____

____

____

____

A prayer to pray today: *Show me Your way, O Lord. Give me courage to think and act like the Christian person You want me to be. Help me make a positive contribution to this world by being an active Christian with convictions. In the name of Jesus, who set a loving, concerned example for us all. Amen.*

You are the salt of the earth. . . . You are the light of the world. . . . Let your light shine before men, that they may see your good deeds and praise your Father in heaven.

Matthew 5:13a, 14a, 16

Session 39

People, People, Hungry People . . .

Julio sits on a street corner in Laredo and begs for food. This five year old boy has five older brothers and sisters who steal every day to help feed their family. Julio's baby sister died last year of malnutrition.

More than half the world's families go to bed hungry. And more people die of hunger in three days than all the people killed in the atomic bomb destruction at Hiroshima, Japan.

Sandy and her mother live wherever they can. They sleep in city parks. They rummage for food scraps from alley dumpsters. They wake up hungry. They live hungry. Sometimes the mother and daughter drink a half cup of soup from a relief kitchen—their sustenance for a few days.

People, people, hungry people! All over the world. Far away. And very close to home.

MY FEELINGS ABOUT WORLD HUNGER

1. Hungry people live everywhere. Are you one of the hungry people in the world? Do you know someone in your family, in your neighborhood, in your school or congregation, who is hungry most of the time?

Sometimes news of hunger on the mass media heightens our awareness of this problem. In 1985 a large group of professional musicians released a popular song, "We Are The World," written by Michael Jackson and Lionel Richie. The proceeds from this song are being directed to a famine relief fund for Africa. It appears that the song will raise more than 100 million dollars! Most of these "USA for Africa" funds will be used for immediate relief, medical care, vaccines, seeds and farm implements, and development of means to generate water and food supplies.

What are your first thoughts when you hear about "the hungry people of the world"?

2. When you hear of people dying of hunger, do you want to blame someone or something? It's easy to put the blame somewhere! Read **Romans 3:9-20** and **3:23.** How do these verses relate to world hunger?

3. Now read **Genesis 1:27-31.** How did God intend the world and its people to be?

4. As one of the world's sinners, in what ways, insignificant and small as they may be, have you perhaps contributed to the world hunger problem?

5. We need not make our own lives less happy to help hungry people. We need not feel guilty about the abundance of blessings we enjoy. We CAN ask God to forgive us for wasting the food and resources He has given us. We CAN ask Him to forgive us for feeling apathetic toward those experiencing hunger, poverty, and pain. In response to God's love and goodness to us, we CAN give to others. We CAN open our hands as Jesus did when He said to the hungry, **"They do not need to go away. You give them something to eat" (Matthew 14:16).**

It's amazing how far a dollar goes. In 1985, if a person in North American gave two dollars, he or she provided a child in Asia with a protein-rich meal everyday for a month. In that same year, five dollars could ship milk to 1,000 children in Africa! We can't solve the world's huge hunger problems by ourselves, but we CAN work together and give generously and consistently in response to God's love through Jesus.

You might set aside a special offering can for the hungry. Each day you could, for example, give five cents for each person in your family that ate well. Send your total offering each month or each quarter to help feed the starving people through LCMS World Relief, 1333 South Kirkwood Road, St. Louis, MO 63122-7295.

WHAT DOES SCRIPTURE SAY?

1. According to **Luke 9:10-17,** how did Jesus feed the 5000 people both spiritually and physically?

---

2. Tell how early Christians fed people according to these passages:

Acts 11:27-30 ______________________

2 Corinthians 9:1-15 ______________________

3. What command does Jesus give to us in **John 13:34?**

____

What does God's love move us to do about the problem of hungry people in the world **(Matthew 25:35, 40, 44, and 45)**?

____

____

4. Now write a brief statement telling your Christian position in our hungry world. Who are you? What does Jesus say to you? And what might your response be to Him and to hungry people?

____

____

____

TEAMING UP AGAINST HUNGER

1. You're aware of the hunger problem. You realize you're not totally to blame. You're free, through Jesus' forgiveness of your own sin, to do something about this worldwide problem. So, WHERE DO YOU START? Pray for a continued awareness of the problem. Pray for God's gifts of understanding and wisdom to do His will in your living. Pray, expecting God to help you, uplift you, and answer your prayers in His time and in His way. Quietly meditate now on the millions of hungry people, on God's love for them, and on His task for you.

2. Remember the words of **John 13:34: "A new commandment I give you: Love one another. As I have loved you, so you must love one another."** This command can seem so general to us, can't it? How can we obey this command of Jesus in relation to the world hunger problem?

LOVE IN ACTION

You might choose to participate in one or more of the following projects to actively demonstrate your feelings and commitments about world hunger. Add your own ideas to this list.

1. Do without one meat-meal per week. Each month, for one year, send the cost of those meals as your offering to LCMS World Relief, 1333 South Kirkwood Road, St. Louis, MO 63122-7295.

2. Encourage your family to plan and prepare meals without meat, substituting other sources of protein. Ask members of your family to also support the fund for the hungry through Lutheran World Relief.

3. Write your opinions about hunger. Write an editorial for your school newspaper. Write your local newspaper. Write your congressional representatives. Write an article for your church newsletter. Let the readers know how you feel about world hunger and share your ideas for helping solve the problem.

4. Remind your family, friends, pastors, and youth group members to pray for hungry people often.

5. Encourage your family and friends to buy two extra canned foods each time they go grocery shopping. Donate the extra food to a local food pantry for the needy.

6. Keep a notebook recording how much food you waste each month. Work to improve your record. Pray for the hungry people especially when you thank God for your blessings of food and drink.

7. Plant a garden at home and share your produce with needy families in your community. Or volunteer to help others (working families, elderly people, single-parent families, etc.) plan and care for their own gardens to increase their food supply. Let your church secretary know of any fresh produce you have to give away so that it might be publicized for needy families in your congregation and community.

8. Decide on a class fund raising activity (perhaps involving your families as well). You might conduct a bake sale, collect a special offering at school or throughout your neighborhood, or present a puppet show at a local shopping center. Publicize well in advance that any fund raising project proceeds will be sent to Lutheran World Relief.

Pray that God will help you contribute to changing this world hunger problem. Thank God for His Holy Spirit, for His blessings of power and confidence for you as you change the world and make it a better place, and for the joy and happiness He gives you through your work.

Whatever you did for one of the least of these brothers of Mine, you did it for Me.

Matthew 25:40

Session 40:

How Can I Reach Others for Christ?

When Jesus tells us to "love one another," what exactly does He mean for us to do?

Can you think of three specific things you could do today that would show someone that Christ lives in you and you live in Him? List them.

REACHING FURTHER, HIGHER, OFTENER, CLOSER . . .

1. Do you think you are racially biased? prejudiced? Do you ever discriminate on the basis of race? And how do you feel about racial prejudice and discrimination among different races in the world? Use Scripture to support your answer if possible.

2. Describe how you feel about the world God made and your part in the ecological caring of the world. Use Scripture to support your answer.

3. Write your views and opinions about nuclear war and describe anything Scripture has to say about war in general.

4. Tell how you view your role within your family. Compare it to the way you see your role within God's family of believers.

5. How do you feel about being a human organ recipient? about being a human organ donor? And how do you feel about medical teams using animal organs for human transplant surgeries? Give Scripture passages to support your answer.

6. Now consider the subject of aging and respecting the elderly in our population. Think of an example from Scripture and describe the elderly person. Tell if he or she was respected and how. Then briefly tell how you can respect the aging people in our society and the process of aging itself.

7. Define "euthanasia." How do you feel about the practice of euthanasia in general? If the life of one of your parents or grandparents depended totally upon a hospital's life-support machine, how would you feel?

8. What are some of your freedoms and privileges? How do you feel about "following the rules" at home, at school, in your country? How does Scripture help us celebrate freedoms?

9. In what ways could you reach out to developmentally disabled people? Find Scripture passages that relate to you and the handicapped, not-so-able people around you.

10. Do you know someone who has not yet been baptized? How can you reach out to that person? What Scripture passages will help you witness Christ's love to him or her?

11. Find Scripture passages that focus on your well-being and care for your body. How can you be a witness to people who use different kinds of drugs and tobacco?

12. How do you think God feels toward the violence and abusive language throughout our media today—TV and radio shows and music, newpaper articles and cartoon commentaries, magazines and books? In what ways can you witness for Christ concerning these problems?

. . .AND CLOSER!

The list of problems and concerns might be endless.

Add your own concerns. And share them with your family and friends. Pray that God will keep you aware of problems, help you be sensitive to others, and show you how you can work in positive ways and be His witness to people.

Jesus gives us a command. The words to a folksong, "Pass My Love Around," tell us our important job. Jesus says:

Pass My love around; pick right up, and take My brother's hand, and pass My love around.

I lived and died to set men free from sin; Now be My presence to all men, Now be My presence to all men.

My word and truth to you I leave behind; Now be My witness to mankind, Now be My witness to mankind.

Teach them to obey everything I have commanded you. And surely I will be with you always, to the very end of the age.

Matthew 28:20

You will be made rich in every way so that you can be generous on every occasion, and through us your generosity will result in thanksgiving to God. This service that you perform is not only supplying the needs of God's people but is also overflowing in many expressions of thanks to God.

2 Corinthians 9:11-12

Unit 8

My Christian Vocation—What Might It Be?

Someone began constructing a large cathedral back in the Middle Ages. One day a visitor walked by the construction site. He asked some of the workers: "What are you doing?"

The first worker replied with a scowl on his face, "I'm putting stones in place! Can't you see?"

The second worker explained, "I'm earning money so that I can take care of my wife and children."

The third worker looked up. His eyes sparkled with joy as he answered excitedly, "What am I doing? I'm building a cathedral!"

How do you look at your life? Is it dull and boring? Does it seem practical, but not too interesting? Or is your life happy most of the time? Throughout this unit, you'll discover what God has to tell you about your daily living, about choosing a job—a vocation—and how He can help you be the happy Christian worker He wants you to be!

Session 41

Servants and Vocations

"What do you want to BE when you grow up?" Grandpa asked me each time I visited him in the country. When I was four years old, I answered, "I'm gonna be a waitress at Arby's!" When I was ten years old, I replied, "Grandpa, I'd like to be a space shuttle astronaut!" And now I'm fourteen years old. And now I'm not sure WHAT I want to be in a few years. I'm really confused!

You don't have to decide on a vocation immediately. Choosing important things like that take a lot of time and thought! While you're thinking about your own future, remember that your life is God's gift to you. What you do in and with your life is your response to God.

WHAT IS A VOCATION?

1. Look up the word *vocation* in the dictionary and write a definition in your own words.

____

____

2. Do you have a vocation now? What do you think God wants you to do with your life?

____

____

3. God probably won't miraculously show you what He wants you to "be" on the day you graduate from high school. The decision might be very difficult for you. It's important for you to begin to honestly evaluate your abilities, your interests, and your possibilities in a Christian way. It's important that you be open to God's guidance for you.

WHAT IS A SERVANT?

Throughout Scripture, the vocation of servant is one that stands out. A servant, in the sense used in this unit, is someone who willingly gives of himself or herself for the good of someone else.

1. What are your first thoughts when you hear the word "servant"?

____

2. God looks at a servant in a very positive way. He wants us to be His servants. Read these Scripture passages and describe the "servant" and his or her action.

Isaiah 42:1-4 ______________________

Luke 12:35-40 ______________________

Matthew 11:29-30 ______________________

Matthew 20:26-28 ______________________

Hebrews 3:5 ______________________

1 Corinthians 4:6-13 ______________________

3. Jesus is the best example of a servant—our servant. God chose Him, loves Him, and is very pleased with His work! We can say the same about us: God chooses us, He loves and cares for us, and He helps us serve. We respond to God by serving other people in our daily lives. Read **Matthew 12:15-21.** Tell in what ways Jesus is our servant.

____

____

MY SERVANTHOOD

1. Read **1 Corinthians 10:31.** Circle the following actions that you can do as a servant that would glorify God:

eat watermelon
watch TV
read a book
smoke a cigarette
wash the family car
play basketball
overeat
fight with your neighbor
go to church

2. Read **Philippians 2:1-8.** How can you *really* be like Jesus? What is Paul saying to the Philippians about being Christians? ____________________

____

3. Read **John 13:2-9.** Why do you think Jesus washed His disciples' feet? How can we "wash people's feet" in our daily living? ____________________

____

4. List five jobs in which you think you could happily serve God and people. ____________________

____

5. List five jobs in which you feel sure you could not serve God and people. ____________________

____

6. I think that my relationship with God helps me in these ways: ____________________

____

WHAT JOB IS MOST IMPORTANT?

1. Rank the following jobs from 1 to 10. Number 1 would mean the most important job in your opinion; number 10 would be the least important job.

__Police officer	__Carpenter	__Surgeon
__Pastor	__Truck driver	__Secretary
__Computer programmer	__U.S. President	__Auto mechanic
	__Lutheran school teacher	

Was it hard to rank these vocations in an order of importance? Could you agree that many jobs can be done to the glory of God?

2. Describe the person you would most like to be like and tell why. ____________________

____

3. Write a short paragraph telling in what vocation you look forward to working, and why.

____

____

____

____

A prayer to pray today: *Dear God, You have given me all that I am and have. I thank You. And I ask you to please help me be Your servant to other people around me—in school, in sports activities, in creative arts, in my family life, and in my neighborhood. Please help me do all that I do to Your glory and honor. In Jesus' name. Amen.*

Whoever wants to become great among you must be your servant, and whoever wants to be first must be your slave—just as the Son of Man did not come to be served, but to serve, and to give His life as a ransom for many.

Matthew 20:26-28

Session 42

Square Pegs and Round Holes

Did you ever watch a small child play with a preschool toy and try to fit a block into a round hole?

Or have you dreamed of being a video star when, perhaps, you'll someday sell and repair video equipment instead?

Finding your "niche" in life isn't easy.

What is your call? What is your "niche"? And how can you, as a high school student, lend a hand and fit into a position as a servant? Let's discover in this session something about talents and how to use them.

WHAT GOD GAVE US

1. According to **Genesis 1:26-31**, what did God give us? And how did God feel about all the things and people He created?

____

____

2. Read the parable of the three servants in **Matthew 25:14-30.**

a. What did each servant receive?

Servant 1: ______________________

Servant 2: ______________________

Servant 3: ______________________

b. What did each servant do with the money entrusted to him?

Servant 1: ______________________

Servant 2: ______________________

Servant 3: ______________________

c. What reward or punishment did each servant receive?

Servant 1: ______________________

Servant 2: ______________________

Servant 3: ______________________

3. What "talents" has God entrusted to you? How do you use them? And in what ways does God reward you?

____

____

____

WHAT THE WORLD NEEDS

1. List some things you think the world needs.

____

____

2. The world needs caring people. People who care about each other. God cared so much for us all that He sent Jesus to save us from sin **(John 3:16).** God expects us to care for each other as Jesus cares for His brothers and sisters here on earth. This is one way that I can show that I care for someone else: ___

____

3. The world needs dedicated people. People who give to others unselfishly. People who are dedicated to God and to their work. Jesus was dedicated to His work: saving us! Dedicated people do MORE than just the average work. They demonstrate faithfulness, kindness, Christian love, and respect for people around them. This is one way that I can show that I'm dedicated to others:

____

____

____

WHAT'S MY COMMITMENT?

1. Read **Luke 16:10-13.** You are given a choice between serving two masters. As a Christian, to whom are you loyal?

____

2. In this loyalty, why is it important that you look at the motivation behind a vocation?

____

____

3. Think about spending most of your time at a job. Think about the characteristics of the job and how important each one is to you. Now read the list and rank the characteristics from 1 (very important) to 5 (not important at all). (Note that several jobs could be ranked the same.)

____My job gives me freedom to be myself—a moral person.

____My job provides opportunities for me to travel a lot.

____My job allows me to be my own boss.

____My job lets me be a servant to others.

____My job assures me that I'll make enough money to do anything I like.

____My job provides opportunities to attain higher level jobs and pay.

____My job means I'll never have to take home work.

Be prepared to share your ranking of job characteristics with your class.

4. How is having a vocation more than having just an occupation? ______________________________

____

____

5. Think of a special job and commit yourself to fulfilling it during this next week. Choose a job that reflects, in some way, a role of a servant to others. Complete the following commitment.

I, ______________ *promise to serve God and people during the next week by* ______________

____

____

____

____

Signed ______________

(God's servant)

A prayer to pray today: *I thank You, Lord, for the variety of jobs you've already given me. Give me patience, love, kindness, and a forgiving attitude toward others. Keep me humble and help me to care as I serve You daily. Through Jesus' love and for His sake I pray. Amen.*

No servant can serve two masters.

Luke 16:13

Take My yoke upon you and learn from Me, for I am gentle and humble in heart, and you will find rest for your souls. For My yoke is easy and My burden is light.

Matthew 11:29-30

There are different kinds of gifts, but the same Spirit. There are different kinds of service, but the same Lord. There are different kinds of working, but the same God works all of them in all men.

1 Corinthians 12:4-6

Session 43

Do I Have a Choice?

Which flavor of ice cream would you choose—peanut brittle or jamoca fudge? What's your favorite color of sports car? And if you could paint your bedroom any color you like, what color would you choose?

We all make choices each day. Some are more crucial than others. Many are routine choices. What will I eat for breakfast? What will I pack in my lunch bag? What will I wear to the cinema? Making choices is a part of living. And making choices allows us freedom to grow and mature and experiment and learn. In high school, you have some freedom to choose class subjects to prepare for your life after high school. You have the freedom to choose among unlimited vocations for your future. In this session, you'll read and learn more about the importance of making choices, how your choice might be part of your "servanthood," and how God helps you in choosing for your own future.

CHOICES OF BIBLE PEOPLE

1. Read **Luke 5:1-11.** Tell about the people and the choice they made according to this Scripture account.

How did Jesus influence their decision?

2. According to **1 Samuel 3,** what choice did Samuel make, and how did the Lord help him?

3. Read **Acts 10** and **11.** Describe Peter's decision, his actions, and how the Lord helped and blessed him in his choice.

4. Tell how Jesus' disciples chose to work according to **Acts 11:29.**

POPULAR JOBS TODAY

1. List some jobs you think are the most popular in the world today. Tell why you think people tend to choose those jobs. And tell, also, if you think those jobs encourage servanthood.

____

____

____

____

2. Tell why you might choose one of those popular jobs today, and describe how you would be a servant through that job.

____

____

3. According to the parable Jesus told about the talents **(Matthew 25:14-30),** what should you do with the abilities God has given you?

____

____

4. About what does Paul warn the people in **2 Thessalonians 3:10-13**?

____

The world needs a variety of workers today, just as it needed a much different collection of workers a century ago. Today, for example, the demand for assembly line production workers is lessening. But a young person living in the middle of the 1900's probably wouldn't have imagined the opportunities that would change and open in fields like electronics and computers and space technology!

Because the needs of people change so often, it's very important to be a committed *servant.* Living as a *servant* means living as God would like you to live. Committing yourself to serving means that you help others through your *vocation,* and that serving enriches your occupation and makes it much more than just a job.

WHAT ARE MY CHOICES?

God doesn't say that one job is more important than another. He helps you serve through whatever job you might choose. It's only natural that you might like some jobs more than others. You enjoy certain things and do well at them. You have special interests and hobbies.

1. List some of the things that you're interested in and specific things you're good at doing.

____

____

If you've taken an "aptitude test," ask your principal, teacher or counselor to share the results with you. Find out your strengths and weaknesses and build on them.

2. What choices are you free to make through your high school years that will affect your future vocation? Evaluate whether you are honestly applying yourself to your studies, or whether you tend to take the "easy road" and have "fun" most of the time. What's your priority when it comes to learning and preparing for a future job?

____

____

____

____

____

3. It might be hard to determine exactly what you're interested in and what abilities you have. You might have a variety of abilities that could help you be good at a number of different jobs. Read the following descriptions and circle the letters of those that you think describe you in some ways.

a. Mechanically-minded people: These like to fix machines and build things with their hands.

b. Sales-motivated people: These like working with people to make a lot of money; these might like performing, influencing, and working toward a main goal.

c. Analyzers: These people like being faced with problems and solving them; these might like to explore, investigate, and analyze problems.

d. Social-servers: These people enjoy helping other people; they might teach, cure, lead people to better lifestyles, and counsel others.

e. Creative people: These people have artistic abilities; they might write, draw, perform dramatically or musically, and like to have unlimited opportunities to be creative.

f. Logically-minded people: These people like to work with mathematical projects, like detailed work, and have the ability to follow directions completely through in very detailed ways.

g. Outdoor people: These enjoy working outside with plants, animals, and all kinds of nature study.

4. What specific characteristics can you pick out of these groups that describe yourself? List the first and second group that you best fit into:

____

____

5. Tell what occupations could fit into the first and second groups that best describe you. Tell, also, how you might be a *servant* in these jobs.

____

____

____

____

6. As you think about your future vocation, which occupations might be obsolete in the coming years?

____

____

7. List from one to three occupations that you think would be most fulfilling for you and tell why.

____

____

____

8. Do you think any of the occupations you listed would be helpful to the world at large? If so, how?

____

____

9. Write the main ideas from these Scripture passages that relate to you using your God-given talents to the best of your ability:

Colossians 3:12-17 ______________________________

1 Peter 4:8-11 ______________________________

1 Corinthians 10:31 ______________________________

10. As you think seriously about your future vocation, write the advice God gives to you in **Philippians 4:6-7.**

____

Now fear the Lord and serve Him with all faithfulness. . . . choose for yourselves this day whom you will serve . . . . as for me and my household, we will serve the Lord.

Joshua 24:14-15

Session 44

May I Ask Who's Calling?

God: Hello. This is God calling. I love you.

Sinners: I'm busy right now. Call back later.

God: Hello. This is God calling. I love you.

Sinners: I'm too tired to talk right now. I've had a busy day. Call back later when I'm not so tired.

God: Hello. This is God calling. I love you.

Sinners: Don't you ever give up? I sin. I live in sin. I love to sin. Why don't You just leave me alone? I have enough problems now!

God: Hello. This is God. I love you.

Sinners: I'm sorry. I can't accept that. There must be a catch. You want money, don't you? How much will it cost?

God: There is no cost. I just want you to know that I love you.

Sinners: Love me? Prove it! How dc I know you love me?

God: I sent my Son, Jesus, to die for you, to pay the debt that you owe me.

Sinners: Owe you? What do I owe you?

God: Perfection!!

Sinners: That's ridiculous. I can't be perfect!

God: I know! That's why I sent Jesus.

Sinners: Oh, come on! Give up Your Son for me? Why would You do a thing like that?

God: Because I love you. No other reason.

Sinners: I'm sorry. I just can't believe that.

God: Why not? Isn't that good news? Don't you like good news?

Sinners: Yes. But this! It doesn't make any sense. Let me think about it.

God: All right. Think about it. Meanwhile I'll be waiting.

Sinners: Waiting? Waiting for what?

God: You. All of you.

WHO IS CALLING? WHO IS CALLED?

1. Read **Matthew 9:9-13.**

a. Describe Matthew's job when Jesus called him.

____

b. Why do you think Matthew left his job and followed Jesus?

____

____

2. According to **1 John 3:1 and 18,** who calls you? And what are you to be and to do?

3. In what does Jesus make us partners, according to **Hebrews 3:1**?

4. In the final statement of God in the introduction to this session, what do you think the words "all of you" mean?

5. What are some things you think God calls you to do as a high school student? As a future servant in a special vocation?

____

____

MOTIVATIONS, INFLUENCES, AND EXPECTATIONS

1. Circle the things that most likely motivate you to choose a certain job. Add other words as you think of them.

money   power   vacations   travel   hard work
glamour   love   service to others   recognition/fame

2. Tell some ways that other people might influence your career-choice decision. These people might be your parents, your grandparents, other relatives, or teachers and friends. What do you think they *expect* you to be? and why?

____

____

____

____

____

3. Describe what you expect of yourself pertaining to a job. What do you dream about your future? In what

position(s) can you realistically see yourself in the near future?

4. Peter says in **1 Peter 1:13-16** to "hope in Jesus, resist evil desires, and do everything in a way that is pleasing to God." How does this advice relate to you and your making a career-related decision?

FULL-TIME CHRISTIAN VOCATIONS

Could God be calling you right now to serve Him in the world through a church-related Christian vocation?

God "calls" and directs people in various ways. A high school youth visited a new synodical college with a friend and heard the combined choirs and orchestra in concert. This youth told her parents that same evening, "I want to go to that college and major in music. I want to witness to others in the way the college musicians witnessed to me tonight."

1. Who has been the greatest servant in your life so far? In what ways?

2. Complete this sentence: When I think about becoming a full-time church worker (a pastor, a deaconess, a director of Christian education, a day school principal or teacher, for example), I feel

3. What gift do you have right now to serve other people? Read **1 Corinthians 13.** How is this gift so important in your servanthood?

4. Tell why someone would want to be the following servants in full-time church work. What might be their motivation? their expectations? their joys and their sorrows in the job?

a. A pastor:

b. A deaconess:

c. A director of Christian education:

d. A Christian day school principal and/or teacher:

e. A minister of education and evangelism:

f. A minister of youth:

g. A minister of music:

h. A director of early childhood education:

i. A church business administrator:

5. Might God call you into full-time church work through someone else (a pastor, a brother or sister, or a friend for example)? Read **John 1:40-42** to discover how God sometimes calls His people.

6. Choose four words to describe the kind of worker you will be in the next ten years, no matter what vocation or occupation you decide upon. Then briefly tell how God will help you be that worker.

A prayer to pray today: *Dear God, help me to hear Your call to me. Send me Your Holy Spirit, that Your focus might be clear to me for my life. Help me to praise, honor, and please You in all that I do. In Jesus' name. Amen.*

And we know that in all things God works for the good of those who love Him, who have been called according to His purpose.

Romans 8:28

Session 45

God Walks With Me

Once a young boy decided he wanted to be a firefighter. He finished sixth grade, applied for a job at the fire station, and the fire chief told him, "Go and finish high school. Then come back and ask about a job." Within the year he had changed his mind about being a firefighter.

The young man graduated from high school and decided he wanted to be an aeronautical engineer. "To do that work," his counselor advised, "you must go to a good engineering college."

The engineering major graduated *summa cum laude* in his class. He worked for a nationally known aeronautical firm for three years. When his father died, the young engineer chose to change his vocation. He moved to the family's large farm and for ten years he planted and harvested grain crops and raised beef cattle.

One evening, after attending a family Bible study with other friends, this husband and father told his own family, "God is telling me to do something else with my life. I feel that He wants me to become a pastor, and in that way, He will use me and my gifts to tell others about His love."

God walked with this man from his creation throughout the changes in his life. God was with him in each of his dreams and occupations. Just as God loved this man, He loves you as His unique creation. And He will always be with you in new and different situations throughout your life.

You are in charge. Each decision you make is a new beginning for you. Trust in God to guide you and walk with you as you live to serve Him in all that you say and do.

Write in your own words what Jesus promises you in **Matthew 7:7-8** and **Luke 11:9-10.** ____________

____

____

____

____

____

____

LOOKING AT MYSELF ONE MORE TIME

1. Draw a happy face beside the words that describe how you see yourself. Then draw a cross beside the words that characterize a servant of the Lord. You might have two symbols beside the same word! Add more adjectives as you think of them.

energetic	*fickle*	*curious*
generous	*strong*	*normal*
humorous	*weak*	*thoughtful*
practical	*gregarious*	*sensitive*
shy	*talented*	*caring*
kind	*careful*	*creative*
bold	*quiet*	*loyal*
eclectic	*sociable*	*proud*
handsome	*helpful*	

2. Read **Romans 11:33-36.** God has given you EVERYTHING! Name two gifts with which He blesses you:

____

____

In what way can you give these gifts back to God?

____

____

____

3. God loves and accepts you just the way you are. He walks with you in a guiding and accepting way when you're in high school. He will continue to be your Perfect Caregiver in your vocations after high school. Read **Philippians 4:6-7** and describe how you know God is always with you. And how does this make you feel?

____

____

CONCLUSIONS

Read this story. Then use a separate sheet of paper and create an ending for this story. At the same time, think about your own life. Ask the Holy Spirit to lead you in your decision-making concerning your future vocation.

Day of Decision

Passengers on the ship enjoyed themselves on a beautiful day at sea. As they played shuffleboard, swam, and ate delicious foods prepared by French chefs, the balmy air and clear sky reflected in the ocean's glassy waters. "What a wonderful day to be alive!" I thought.

Then it happened. A tremendous explosion rocked the entire ship. Sirens wailed. People screamed. The captain's voice boomed over the public address system, instructing people how to board the lifeboats. People panicked everywhere!

After all the passengers climbed into lifeboats, I could see the captain standing on the bridge, almost as if he were waiting to go down with his ship. Suddenly, a second explosion threw the captain into the water, and a nearby lifeboat rescued him.

Not until then did I wonder, "How far are we from land? And how could we all survive?" Clearly, we all needed a rescue ship soon if we were to survive. On the morning of the third day, our rescue ship appeared, greeted by cheers from the many people. But a curious thing happened when the rescue captain lowered the ship's launch into the water and invited the people to get on board. Many people in the lifeboats decided to look for adventure and try to make it safely to land by themselves! The captain pointed out the folly of such a choice, but to no avail. I couldn't resist his invitation, though, as much as I enjoyed adventure. Soon some of us safely on board waved goodby to those in the tiny boats.

Two days later, a violent storm blew up. We all knew that those adventuresome lifeboat people probably never stood a chance of surviving the storm and making it to land safely.

Three more days passed. As I leaned on a rail and thought about everything that had happened, the captain approached me. "My ship carries no cargo," he explained. "The mission of this ship is to rescue people who need help. And to be able to continue this mission, I have to find funds and more crew members to work with me. Would you help with this rescue project? Would you be my assistant and help recruit crew members and sponsors?"

I stared at the captain. "Why was he asking ME?" I wondered. I said nothing. I just thought about his words.

We reached port the next day. As I walked down the gang plank, I looked back at the ship and caught the captain's eye. He followed me, and then asked, "Well, have you made up your mind yet?"

I looked at him and replied, "______________."

A prayer to pray today: *Dear Lord, bless me and guide me. Show me the way that I can best serve You by using my talents. Give me opportunities to use the gifts You've given to me. Guide me in decision-making concerning my future vocation. And help me develop and commit my gifts to Your service. Help me remember that I can serve You in many different ways. And reassure me that nothing can separate me from Your love. Bless me and walk with me, dear Lord. Amen.*

Who shall separate us from the love of Christ? Shall trouble or hardship or persecution or famine or nakedness or danger or sword? . . . I am convinced that neither death nor life, neither angels nor demons, neither the present nor the future, nor any powers, neither height nor depth, nor anything else in all creation, will be able to separate us from the love of God that is in Christ Jesus our Lord.

Romans 8:35, 38, 39

CPSIA information can be obtained at www.ICGtesting.com
Printed in the USA
LVOW090810311012
305178LV00001B/7/P